My Dad

The Smartest Seventh Grader on Earth

RANDY EUBANKS

PAGE PUBLISHING, INC.
New York, NY

First originally published by Page Publishing, Inc. 2018

ISBN 978-1-64214-879-4 (Paperback)
ISBN 978-1-64298-644-0 (Hardcover)
ISBN 978-1-64214-880-0 (Digital)

Printed in the United States of America

This book is dedicated to my hero my dad
and the smartest 7th grader on earth.

Contents

Chapter 1

Two Years Too Late

Disappointment: The feeling of sadness or displeasure caused by the nonfulfillment of one's hopes or expectations.

Hope: A feeling of expectation and desire for a certain thing to happen.

Growing up on a farm, we always had plenty of food to eat, and all our needs were met; however, we didn't have a lot of money. I would still consider us a middle-class family, but with a twist.

In my younger days, we had no indoor bathroom, so I took a bath in a metal washtub. When you finished bathing, you carried it outside and emptied it. Fortunately, we didn't have to go far as our bathroom was a small wooden building in our backyard. The building was what you called an outhouse. When you walked in, you looked around for spiders and snakes before you sat down to take care of business. Luckily, we didn't have to go outside to urinate. We urinated in a white metal pot located inside of our house. One of my jobs when I came home from school was to take the white urinal pot across the dirt road and dump it into the hogpen. You had to be careful in how fast you walked carrying the urinal pot. You didn't want the urine to splash on your legs.

Let me tell you why we didn't have an indoor bathroom. To start with, it had nothing to do with money or the lack thereof. It was a family issue. And it's complicated.

Years earlier, my granddaddy entertained some of his relatives visiting from Michigan. According to my dad, back in the day when he was growing up, one of their cousins had to use the bathroom while visiting my granddaddy. The relative stopped up the toilet and didn't let my granddaddy know what had happened. Upon them leaving to go back to Michigan, my granddaddy discovered what had happened. He was so upset that he disconnected the indoor toilet and made my dad and his siblings start using the outhouse again and the urinal pot. Since we lived in one of Granddaddy's farmhouses when I was a little boy, we had no indoor bathroom. Even though my family lived in the house, Granddaddy refused to allow my dad to put in a bathroom. What a silly reason for not having an indoor toilet, but it was motivation for my dad to build his own home.

In a few years, my dad was able to save up $2,500. He went to the bank and borrowed $2,500 more. With $5,000, he built a new home with an indoor bathroom. Finally, at the age of ten, I took my first shower. That was a great day.

Now, looking back, I think dumping that urinal pot was a disgusting job, but it paled in comparison to the very first job I had at the ripe young age of six. I will never forget that cool Monday morning on June 28, 1965. My dad walked into my bedroom and asked me if I wanted to work today picking up leaves behind the tobacco harvester. I said sure, why not.

I had no idea of what I was volunteering for.

I looked at the clock; it was 6:00 a.m. My eyes were open, but my brain asleep as per my answer to my dad's question. I went to work that day. I thought I was going through hell.

The big tobacco leaves hit me in the face. The smell of tobacco gum on my face and body was nauseating. The leaves were half as tall as I was. It seemed like the tobacco clips—which hold the picked leaves together in a bundle—were dropping more leaves on the ground than were staying in the clips. The tobacco harvester kept moving down the tobacco rows, and I was struggling walking behind the harvester, trying to keep up and at the same time picking up the leaves that were falling out of the clips. I would put the leaves under my arms, and when I had all the leaves I could tote, I would run up to the moving harvester and drop them in the basket of the croppers so they could send them back up in the tobacco harvester clips.

Thank God for my dad. He made an effort while he was riding the tobacco harvester, picking up some of the leaves that fell out of the clips onto the ground. He would reach over and grab some leaves to put back in his basket. My uncle, cousin, and my brother weren't concerned about my workload. At least my dad had some compassion for his six-year-old son.

His compassion ended the next morning when he came into my bedroom at 6:00 a.m. and said it was time to get up and go pick up more leaves.

"I don't want to go," I said.

He said, "The first day is voluntary, the second day, mandatory."

I wondered what would happen if my dad had met Mr. Long earlier. Would my life have been easier in that tobacco field? My family could have been wealthy, and I wouldn't have had to pick up leaves at 6:00 a.m. Who knows? I do know this: I would not have had as many tobacco leaves to pick up that day and many days to follow because my dad's invention worked.

These thoughts, combined with my dread of another day of picking up tobacco leaves in the dark, were my first experience with disappointment. My dad must have felt the same way nine years earlier after his meeting with Mr. Long.

It was Friday morning in late June of 1956, which was three years before I was born, my dad sat on the doorsteps of Long Manufacturing with his invention in a brown paper bag, waiting for the president of the company to drive up in his white Cadillac.

Dad saw a need to redesign a tobacco harvester clip that wouldn't let go of any of the leaves. The clip was attached to a chain and sprocket system that transported the tobacco leaves upstairs on the tobacco harvester to be removed by the looper, a person who tied the leaves around a five-foot stick. Each harvester clip held four to five leaves of tobacco. One stick would hold several clips of tobacco. Once the stick was full, it was removed from the looping horse—a wooden rack that held the stick while the looper worked—and hung on a metal rack toward the back of the harvester, and then the process started over again. The problem was the clips would frequently let one or more of the leaves fall out and onto the ground as they were being transported up the chain.

One Thursday in late June during lunch break, my dad designed a new clip that didn't drop any of the leaves. In thirty minutes he had a clip that was a better design than what the college-educated engineers at Long Manufacturing had created. With only a seventh-grade education, and a lot of common sense and intelligence, my father had outdone the pros.

They had finished putting in tobacco that late Thursday evening. The next morning, my dad drove the two hours to Tarboro, North Carolina, to get there around 8:00 a.m., starting time for any good business. He went inside in hopes of talking to the president of Long Manufacturing about his new tobacco harvester clip.

Mr. Long's secretary told my dad that her boss wasn't in and it wouldn't be possible to see him.

"He is a busy man," she said. "Once he's in the office you can forget seeing him. There are appointments scheduled all day."

But there was a solution. The best way to talk to him was to catch him as soon as he drove up and got out of his car before he entered the building. Mr. Long usually drives up around 8:30 a.m. in his white Cadillac.

My dad took her advice. He went outside and sat on the steps to wait on Mr. Long. Soon, Dad noticed a white Cadillac pulling into the parking lot. He headed toward the vehicle as Mr. Long was parking into his marked parking space, and as soon as Mr. Long got out of the car, my dad approached him.

Daddy introduced himself as a farmer and told Mr. Long that he had designed a tobacco harvester clip that was more efficient than the ones they designed and installed on their Long tobacco harvesters.

"Take it out of the bag and show it to me," Mr. Long said.

My dad handed it over, and he took a look at it while they were walking toward his office. He told Daddy by looking at his design, he saw the mistake his engineers had made. He asked Daddy to come in. As they walked by his secretary, he told her to cancel all his appointments for the morning. Over the next four hours, the pair discussed this new design of the tobacco clip.

Mr. Long told Daddy, "Mr. Eubanks, you are two years too late. We are in the process of developing our automatic croppers. Two years sooner on this design, you would have been a rich man. However, I do not want anyone else to have this. I will pay you five hundred for it right now and patent it myself. I will give you a job in the company, send you to school, and give you a percentage on all new inventions and redesigns you come up with."

My dad took the five hundred, but turned down the job and school opportunity. He was a farm boy, and his father was dependent on him to oversee the farm operations; he couldn't just walk away from family. This was Dad's first invention, and he received good compensation for his thirty minutes of effort. This launched his journey of fifty-seven years of inventing and designing items to make our lives easier.

HARVESTER CLIP

W. R. LONG - Pres.
Telephone 2120

LONG manufacturing company, inc.

manufacturers of

TARBORO, NORTH CAROLINA

TOBACCO HARVESTERS ◆ TOBACCO CURERS ◆ HAY BALERS

November 8, 1956

Mr. Furney Eubanks
Route #2
Trenton, North Carolina

Dear Mr. Eubanks:

I am having a contract agreement drawn up on the harvester clip that you designed and it will be necessary for us to file an application for this clip. As soon as I receive these papers, I will forward them to you for your signature and then I will give you a check for $500.00 as agreed upon.

Trusting this is the information you desire and with kind regards, I am

Yours very truly,

LONG MANUFACTURING CO., INC.

W. R. Long
President

WRL/jpp

W. R. LONG · Pres.
Telephone 2120

TARBORO, NORTH CAROLINA

manufacturers of TOBACCO HARVESTERS ♦ TOBACCO CURERS ♦ HAY BALERS

December 29, 1956

Mr. Furnel Eubanks
Route #2
Trenton, North Carolina

Dear Mr. Eubanks:

On November 6th I advised you that I was having a contract
agreement drawn up on the harvester clip that you designed
and that I would let you know when the papers were sent to
me for your signature.

My patent attorney in Washington, D. C., has returned this
application to me and it is now ready for your signature.
I will appreciate very much your coming to Tarboro on January
7th to meet with me and sign this application in order that
I might give you a check in the amount of $500.00 as agreed
upon.

Thanking you and with regards, I am

Yours very truly,

LONG MANUFACTURING CO., INC.

W. R. Long
President

WRL/jpp

Chapter 2

Why Not Sit and Work
at the Same Time?

I remember growing up that my dad was always tinkering on stuff in his shop at night. His first invention that caught my attention happened one Saturday morning in April of 1978. I had married in January of the same year and came back home to visit.

To set the narrative straight, prior to getting married back in the day, I was the last child living at home. One of my chores in a list of many was to keep our big yard mowed. Daddy had purchased a push lawn mower years earlier to help me to accomplish this task. This mower had a twenty-four-inch cutting deck, and it would take me all day to mow the grass. It was a hard job. During the summer, I mowed it every week, and I dreaded it every week for years. Imagine my surprise on that cool April morning when I arrived at my daddy's house and saw him sitting on a brand-new riding lawn mower with a forty-eight-inch mowing deck. To add insult to injury, he had rigged up a brace and attached it to the back right side of the riding lawn mower. Attached to that brace was my old twenty-four-inch push mower. In essence, my dad was mowing seventy-two inches in one swoop around the yard. I couldn't believe it. Not only was he riding, but he had figured out a way to pull my old push lawn mower behind him.

I stopped him and asked, "Why didn't you buy this new riding lawn mower and attach the push mower to it when I was home mowing the grass all those years?"

He quietly said, "There was no need to, I had you here to mow the grass."

That's the way my dad is. He's always looking and thinking of ways to make people's lives easier and saving them time. This was his driving force for his inventions. What used to take me all day to mow the yard, he was now mowing it in two hours. In this case, he looked for ways to save himself time.

This mower attachment was just the beginning. Over the next several years, he and I shared experiences together in which he invented different gadgets as a result of different needs that I had in my business career.

I went into the painting and remodeling business in 1982, and Dad would occasionally come to my job site and observe us working. One particular morning, we were painting the exterior of a two-story house in Pollocksville. Dad had gotten out of the farming business and had pursued a career in upholstery work. He was delivering furniture to a customer down the street and stopped by to see me and my crew. We had our tall ladders stretched out on the side of the house and were scrapping off loose paint and applying primer on the woodwork.

He stood there and watched us climb up the ladder and work at that spot for a few minutes; we then climbed down the ladder and moved it to the next spot. He watched this climbing up and down the ladder for a long time before he spoke up.

He said, "You're wasting time. I am going to work on something to make your life easier and to save you time."

He did. In a couple of months, we tried out his elevatable workstation. He designed a wheelchair-like apparatus in which you sat down to work.

Here is what you would do. You would first extend a tall ladder on the side of the building you were working on. You would then attach a pulley and winch system to the top of the ladder. Two wheels on the chair allowed the seated worker to move up and down the side of the building by simply rotating the wheels. Instead of wasting time moving the ladder back and forth numerous times, you simply set up the ladder and worked from the top all the way down to the ground before you had to move the ladder. This invention saved countless man-hours. Another benefit included sitting on your butt working instead of walking up and down on a ladder all day, which was tiresome to your feet and legs.

This was a great invention that I used for years. My dad got it patented in 1986 and called several companies in pursuit of a manufacturer who might catch the vision and potentially make it for us. I showed it to local paint and hardware stores. Everyone thought it was a great idea, but no company wanted to build it while in the meantime pay us a royalty.

U.S. Patent   Dec. 23, 1986   Sheet 1 of 2   4,630,710

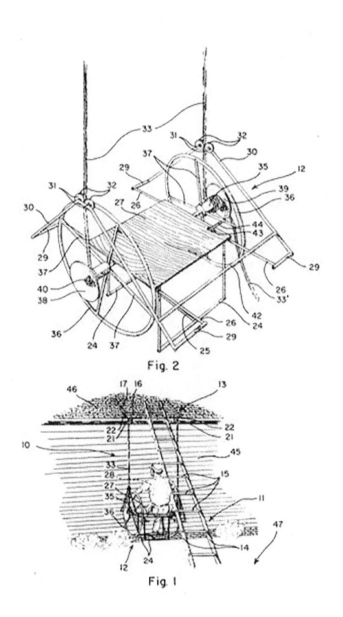

Fig. 2

Fig. 1

We got our hopes up because this was a great invention that worked, but in the end, we were disappointed because we couldn't sell it to a company. Oh well, back to the drawing board. My dad never gave up. He said winners don't quit.

He said, "Let's keep plugging away. Next"

Chapter 3

This Invention Is Going to Be a Winner

I just knew that the next invention was going to be a winner. I had that feeling. Once again, my dad came out to the job site and saw one of my painters working outside with a paint scraper taped to the end of an extension roller pole. My dad asked why he was doing that. The painter told him it makes it easier to tape the scraper to the end of the pole to be able to reach higher places, saving you from climbing up a ladder.

My dad pondered what he had just seen. He went on the inside of the house and observed another painter with a paintbrush taped to the end of an extension roller pole. The painter was standing on the steps in a stairwell, painting a hard-to-reach corner where he couldn't set up an extension ladder. Daddy asked me about this technique of taping paintbrushes and various other tools to an extension roller pole.

"How often do you do this?" he asked.

"We do it all the time," I said. "We are constantly having a need to attach a tool to the end of an extension roller pole."

This made our work easier by saving time and helping us to reach in hard-to-get-to places. The only problems were it was a hassle to cut the tape off and eventually the tape would give, forcing us to retape tools. We were limited by the strength of the duct tape in how much pressure we could exert in using this setup.

Daddy said, "Let me work on it. I will make your life easier."

He worked countless hours in his workshop until he came up with a tool holder design he was happy with. In a few weeks, he invited me over to show off his new invention. I was excited in anticipation of what he had made. Not to my surprise, when I laid my eyes on it, I said, "You did it again. You are a genius."

He said, "No, I am not a genius, but I have common sense. I just know how to create a better way of doing things. I see a need, and I am obsessed with designing a product to address the need. In this case, you had a need to be able to attach a tool on the end of an extension handle in order to save you time and to be able to reach into hard to get to places in order to accomplish your work."

I was impressed. My dad had invented a multipurpose tool holder for extension handles.

He had used a five-foot aluminum pole, and on the end of that pole he had welded a small pivoting plate which the tool would rest against. The tool was held securely in place on the plate by a small cable that wrapped around it. The cable was tightened around the tool by leveraging it with a threaded bolt with a big wing nut on the end. You simple slid the tool between the cable and plate and secured in place by rotating the wing nut, tightening the cable and pressing the tool firmly against the plate. This let the user put all kinds of pressure on the handle, which allowed you to efficiently use the tool holder without worrying about the tool working itself loose. What an ingenious invention.

I knew this was it. We were going to hit the jackpot.

He said, "We can't show it, and you can't use it on the job until I get it protected from someone stealing the idea."

He made me promise not to tell a soul about his invention until it was protected, and as much as I wanted to use it, I agreed.

Daddy had already spent thousands of dollars and who knows how much time obtaining two patents on his elevatable workstation a few years earlier. He said we need to see if we could find an organization to help us in this process.

"Maybe there are grants available for entrepreneurs and inventors through the community college or other organizations," he said.

I told him that I would make some calls. The next day, I went by to see the director of the small business center at Coastal Carolina Community College in Jacksonville, North Carolina. After I described the product to her, she directed me to the small business center in Kinston, North Carolina, where they were set up to deal with entrepreneurs who came up with new products.

I called the folks in Kinston and set up a meeting with me and Dad. It was a great meeting, and the director was impressed with the tool holder. He called the main office in Raleigh and made us an appointment to speak with the man in charge of helping inventors to patent their product and help them in contacting or marketing to companies who might have an interest in manufacturing and distributing the product. The man's name was Dr. Fred Carr. We set an appointment to see Dr. Carr, and though he was busy, we set an appointment for a few weeks out. In the meantime, Daddy had filed a temporary form with the Patent Office, which would get his invention temporarily protected while he was in the process of fully protecting it by filing a patent. He had one year to get it protected before his temporary protection ran out, and since he was protected good enough in the short run, he started showing his product. Not only did we start showing the tool holder, we did one better than that: we made a slew of them.

I came over in the afternoons and helped him build the extension tool holders in his workshop. We manufactured them ourselves and even ordered stickers to put on them, advertising our new makeshift manufacturing company. We didn't have an official name of a company, but we called it Furney Eubanks extension tool holder. In his little workshop, we made over 115 of the tool holders.

Daddy and I convinced hardware and paint stores to display and sell them on consignment. We were able to sell the 115 poles, and they were sold in Trenton, Kinston, New Bern, and as far away as Raleigh. A couple of national chains like Glidden and Sherwin Williams paint stores were some of the stores we put them in. The stores retailed them for $14.95 each, and we were wholesaling them to the stores for $10.00. We soon discovered this was not the route we wanted to go. It was taking too much of our time, and we weren't set up to mass-produce and market them.

After a few weeks of this, we were able to meet with Dr. Carr. We were excited to finally meet Dr. Carr and start working with him. His job was as the overseer of a program designed to help small businesses get off the ground with new inventions. The goal of this program was to provide grant money which could lead to increase entrepreneur development of products. This, in turn, would create more jobs and help further stimulate the economy. These state grants help to fund the expenses incurred by the entrepreneurs in developing their products.

Dr. Carr was a highly intelligent man who took interest in Daddy and his tool holder. He looked it over and thought it was a wonderful design that had great potential. He said he could see it being manufactured and distributed all over the country and took it upon himself to write the patent for Daddy's invention. He had written patents before, and he was an expert on how the process worked. We were able to save thousands of dollars in attorney fees by using this service offered by the Small Business and Technology Development Center located in Raleigh.

Along with Dr. Carr writing and filing the application for the patent, he was going to help us by getting us in contact with a company which would possibly be interested in manufacturing and selling the tool holder. As per the patent application, the official name of the tool holder would now be called multipurpose tool holder for extension handle. We just kept calling it the tool holder for short.

Dr. Carr filed the application on May 5, 1988. The patent was issued on August 8, 1989. In the meantime, Dr. Carr wrote a letter on our behalf and personally talked to Bill Bryant, who was in charge of the Product Development Department for Empire Brush Company. At the time, Empire Brush Company was one of the biggest manufacturers in the United States of push brooms, scrub brushes, and related products.

Daddy and I were excited about the opportunity of meeting Bill Bryant. Dr. Carr had informed him of our new invention, and he had expressed to Bill that this product might complement their other products and would be a good fit for them. In the letter to Bill Bryant, Dr. Carr attached the patent application for his review. He was very interested in looking at our product. Bill called Daddy and set up an appointment. Dad and I were excited. We just knew this was going to be our big break. We had tested the market, and we determined there was a need just by our own limited sales and marketing. We imagined what a company the size of Empire Brush could do with this product. My dad imagined buying himself a brandnew pickup truck with plush leather seats. He imagined finally being able to put brick on his plywood siding home that he had constructed back in 1969 with limited funds. My imagination ran wild with what that royalty money would buy me. I had in mind buying a yacht and hiring a captain to drive my family and me across the Atlantic Ocean to explore Europe and Italy. I imagined being able to buy and pay cash for a brand-new RV and travel across the country with no set time to return home. I imagined having enough money in the bank to never worry about working again. We couldn't wait.

APPLICATION FOR UNITED STATES LETTERS PATENT

TITLE: MULTI-PURPOSE TOOL HOLDER FOR EXTENSION HANDLE

INVENTOR: Furney Eubanks
                Randy Eubanks

FRED K. CARR
Small Business and Technology
   Center
Raleigh, NC 27605

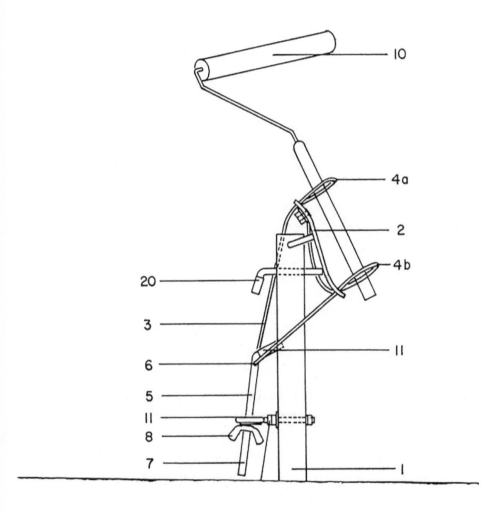

FIG. I

Chapter 4

Why Did They Keep It Two Years?

Daddy and I drove to Greenville that morning with great anticipation of meeting with Bill Bryant. We arrived at Empire Brush Company around 8:30 a.m. for our 9:00 a.m. appointment, early as usual because Daddy didn't like to be late. His theory was if you are not going to be early there is no need to show up.

The receptionist asked us to sit in the reception area and Bill would be out in a few minutes. She offered us a cup of coffee to sip on. Finally, after a few minutes, Bill came out and introduced himself. We went into his office.

After a few minutes of small talk, we got down to business. He had reviewed the patent application that Dr. Carr had sent, and he was eager to see the product. I left it in the car because I didn't want to bring it in for everyone to see. I went back out to get it and brought it back into his office. He looked over the aluminum pole with the odd attachment at the head. Daddy inserted the paintbrush I had brought into the holder, and Bill tested it out. Bill went to the back room and found a bucket of paint. Daddy and I couldn't believe what we were seeing. Bill started painting in the storage room next door to his office. He took the aluminum pole with the tool holder attached and dipped the brush into the paint bucket. He stood on the ground and started painting around the top edge of the wall next to the ceiling. I guess he wasn't concerned that the paint in the bucket didn't match the paint on the wall. It seemed like he was painting for fifteen minutes. He acted like a kid in a candy store. Daddy and I looked at each other and smiled. I thought to myself, "We have got Bill sold." He was impressed.

When he finally put it down, he said, "I tell you, the design's a little rough, but I think there's something our engineers could do with this. I'm willing to make you an offer."

At first, all we heard was "design is rough," and we thought we heard disappointment, but then it hit us: they wanted to build a prototype in which it could be manufactured and marketed in mass production.

Bill ended up sending to the engineering department the patent application along with the tool holder we had brought to the office. Daddy had made the tool holder in combination with the extension pole. It was all-in-one. Bill's idea was to just make the tool holder part with a threaded slot on the bottom of it in which you could screw on to any type of extension pole. This was what we were going to get patented: the holder itself, not the extension pole.

EMPIRE BRUSH COMPANY HAND CARVED PROTOTYPES OF MULTI-PURPOSE
TOOL HOLDER

 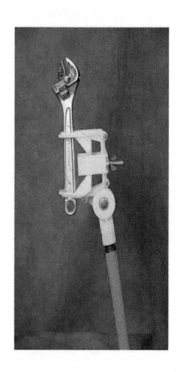

Getting the prototype was a long process, and it took more than six months for the engineering department to get the tool holder prototype finished. An engineer ended up hand carving two prototypes out of plastic, each with a slightly different design. The reason for the two designs was to give the marketing division options for their upcoming testing of the tool holder from their focus groups. The focus groups would now have two options in which they could choose which model they liked the best. Both prototypes accomplished the same thing with a slight different feel. Bill called us in to get our opinion on the models.

We met Bill at his office. On the drive to Greenville, Dad and I discussed what we thought the designs would look like. Honestly, we had no idea they were going to end up making them out of a hard plastic. We finally arrived, and Bill's secretary told us to go back and see Bill. He was expecting us. When we walked into his office, Bill was smiling, and the two prototypes were on top of his desk. Dad grabbed one, and I grabbed the other model. We were overwhelmed with emotion. "Wow," we both said. Finally, a company was taking my dad's inventions seriously. We teared up with emotion. We were impressed with both of them. They were beautiful. What was more impressive was that Bill told us it cost Empire Brush Company ten thousand dollars to pay the engineers to hand carve these two prototypes.

The next step was to send the models to focus groups in order to get market reactions. They wanted to know if there would be a market to sell them nationally and get an idea on the potential number of units they could sell nationwide. This meant it was time to send the models to the marketing department. Once marketing had an idea of the sales potential, they would go to work on figuring the cost of making the molds to mass-produce the tool holders. Which meant the accounting and manufacturing departments got involved.

All in all, they worked on these processes for two years.

We were starting to get impatient, but all the while, Bill was reassuring us that it takes time to get all the data together in order to make a logical decision on whether it would be worth their while to buy it from us. In the meantime, no money had changed hands. Even though Empire Brush Company haven't offered us any upfront money, we knew they were invested in this process since they had by now spent several thousand dollars of their own money to test our tool holder. We still felt confident they would manufacture and sell our product and the money would flow in due time.

What reassured us the most was Bill's excitement about the tool holder. Especially since he would have a lot of input in the final decision on whether to build it or not since he was in charge of new product development. His job was to find new products that would give his company an edge on market share. He was always looking for the next innovative product that would give them a leg up on the competition. And there was someone like him in every big company out there, which meant Bill would have some pressure to buy, even if it was only to keep the tool holder out of the hands of his competition.

We talked about the potential of upfront money plus paying us a royalty on each unit sold. Bill said if they decided to build it, the legal department would handle all the details. Bill couldn't give us any information on how much the upfront money would be and what percentage on each unit they would pay us. He did say this, "You and your dad will be happy." When that time came, Dr. Carr would help make recommendations for the legal counsel we'd need to proceed in this process.

Bill's words of reassurance encouraged us that this was the big break that we had hoped for. My daddy was going to be famous and rich. We could feel it. We were hopeful, and the rest of the family was excited. We kept in contact with Bill over the next few months as the process continued. It felt like an eternity. Each department would pass it on to the next and then to the next, and it never ended. Bill said they got good feedback from the focus groups.

We were eagerly waiting on Bill to give us the final word that Empire Brush was going to build the tool holder when we got a call from Bill. Bill called me and said, "Randy, I have got something to tell you. I have been promoted within the company to another department." I congratulated him and said, "How does your promotion affect our tool holder?" He said, "It's out of my hands, and a new guy will be in charge of product development. I don't know who that new guy is yet, but he will be briefed on the progress of the tool holder and be in touch."

This turned out to be great for Bill but not good for us. The person who filled his position as director of new product development had no interest in our tool holder. Disappointment had reared its ugly head again for my daddy. After more than two years of keeping our product off the market and hindering us from pursuing other options; after Empire Brush Company spent tens of thousands of dollars on engineering, marketing, and focus group fees; after Bill's reassurances and my dreams of riches, it came to nothing. If only Bill had not been promoted or had just been promoted a couple of months later, the end results might have been different for us. But "should'a, would'a, could'a'" and "what if" won't change reality.

It seemed unfair Daddy couldn't catch a break on his inventions. I was especially disappointed on this one because I had spent so much time on helping him with this process.

"What do we do now?" I asked him one day.

We were in his workshop, and he put down the piece he was working on, wiped his hands, and looked at me. "We're going to move on and invent something else. Next."

Next. That's my dad. He never gives up; he just works on what's next. But what was next? Something new? Daddy didn't know of any more companies to contact concerning the multi-purpose tool holder, so he was right. Next. It was time to move on.

Some good news came out of working with Empire Brush. In the process of making and selling these tool holders and in dealing with Empire Brush Company, my dad and I enjoyed a lot of quality time working on a common goal as a father and son. That in itself made it profitable.

In the same way Daddy says "Next," I have always said we need to enjoy the journey. You shouldn't always measure success by the end result but in how you experienced the journey. I have always tried to enjoy the process, and I truly enjoyed the process of working alongside my dad, partnering together toward a goal of accomplishing something worthwhile. It was only a matter of time before my dad saw a need to improve another product.

Chapter 5

The Roller Pole Button

Dad turned his attention to the roller poles we were using at work. He noticed that a lot of the buttons used to lock the pole in place when it was extended broke pretty quickly.

He noticed these buttons because I drove my van up to his upholstery shop one day wanting him to give me a price on recovering my driver's seat. I said, "How much will you charge me to recover my driver's seat on my van." He laughed and said, "You haven't paid me for recovering your couch and chair that I did a couple of years ago, why should I waste my time giving you an estimate on recovering the van seat?" The truth of the matter is my dad wouldn't accept any money from any of his children for recovering their furniture. While he was looking at my driver's seat, he happened to look in the back of the van and saw the roller poles hanging on a rack. "These buttons, why do they break so fast?" he asked.

"Throwing the poles around in the back of the van causes the buttons to pop off," I said. "But they also just break from use."

He thought on it for a minute and said, "There must be a better way to design the button so it doesn't protrude out. No wonder the buttons get knocked off."

Dad went to work in his shop. In a few days, he approached me with his replaceable roller pole button. It was a metal button with a notch welded on it that slips on the hole in the pole to lock it in place. It was secured with a spring that made a loop in order to slide it onto the pole and secure it in place. With Daddy's replacement button, you didn't have to buy a new extension pole when you broke the button; you just replaced the button. It was a handy little device, and I used his extension pole buttons quite frequently.

Daddy didn't go to the expense of getting a patent on this device; instead we showed it around to various paint and hardware stores and the managers in the stores thought it was a good idea, but not something they could sell. Daddy contacted a few companies but never got any interest in manufacturing it. Since then the manufacturers have improved their buttons and you can't knock them off now. I am not sure if they stole his idea or not, but now there are a variety of buttons and other means available to lock extension poles in place. The reason I am suspicious is because I know how these store managers are who work for franchise paint stores. They want to get promoted. I can see one of them trying to impress their regional boss. After I showed them our roller pole button, one of them could have told their regional manager that they had an idea on improving the roller pole button since painters always complained how easy it was to knock them off. The regional manager could have passed it on to corporate, and corporate passed it on to their research and development department. The next thing you know, it's on the market. Who knows? I am just saying.

The next invention he created was a paint can holder. We would use a metal bail—a simple twist of heavy wire—to hook around the metal loop on the paint bucket and then hang it from a ladder rung. Dad didn't like the way it worked, so he invented the paint can holder.

The paint can holder was a neat little device, but personally I didn't have any interest in it. I liked the simple hook that you could buy at any hardware store. Dad thought it had potential, and he used it a lot. He even had a brochure made up advertising it. He never sold any, but many people thought it was a clever idea.

Paint Can

Paint Can + Holder

Not just for Painters. If you can put it in a bucket and you need it on a ladder, this is for you !

- Fits most any ladder
- Hangs on left or right side without adjustment
- Top of the container is clear for easy access
- Needs only one hand to move it to a new position on the ladder
- Attachment hook remains level for easy moving
- Stops on the handle make sure the container remains level while moving but is out of the way while Working

Screws

Once you've tried one You'll never want to be on a ladder without it again!

Chapter 6

Rotten Potatoes Stink

Remember back at my surprise of my dad attaching the push lawn mower to the back of the riding mower? Well, Daddy wasn't finished modifying his riding lawn mower, but this time he set his eyes on the garden. It was a big one, and he loved to work in it, but being tight with money, when he needed a small tractor to plow the garden, he decided to tackle the problem in the workshop.

Growing up, one of my jobs was picking up potatoes in the garden. At that time, Daddy and Granddaddy had a huge garden together on the back side of the farm. The challenge to me was that in my eyes, my dad always overplanted. We never had just enough for our family and a neighbor or two; he planted enough potatoes to feed the neighborhood. Not only did I have to pick up the potatoes when we dug them up, but in the winter I had to sort the good potatoes from the bad.

The potatoes were stored in wooden baskets the size of a five-gallon bucket. Over time, some of the potatoes would start to rot. Remember that saying, "One rotten apple can spoil the whole bunch?" I found out that's true. In this case, one rotten potato can speed up the process of rotting the whole basket if you don't remove the rotten ones.

My job consisted of pouring the basket of potatoes out onto a burlap sheet, then spreading them out so I could find and remove the rotten ones. It wasn't hard to find the rotten potatoes; just follow the smell. As a young boy, I thought that was the worst job in the world. The stench was almost unbearable. It smelled like rotten sewage. In fact, I hated that job. I hated it so badly that I remember going to see my grandmother who lives across the street and complaining to her about how I hated picking up potatoes and my dad and I didn't get along concerning this job. I didn't like picking up all those potatoes out of the garden because I knew come wintertime that a lot of them would rot and be wasted and I would be the one who had to endure the smell.

I was just a nine-year-old boy when I complained to my grandmother, and she must have been quite amused at my complaint because she enjoyed telling it to my Uncle Wayne who owned a little country store in our community. I remember going to the store soon after I had talked to my grandmother. Uncle Wayne piped up as soon as I walked in the store.

"How are you and your dad getting along concerning you picking up potatoes?" he asked, laughing.

My Uncle Wayne never forgot anything. Years later, when I was a grown man, I would stop by and visit Uncle Wayne when I came to visit my parents. He would ask me the same question: "Are you and your dad getting along concerning you picking up potatoes?"

We would laugh together, and I would say, "Thank God, my picking-up-potato days are over."

Since then, my dad has scaled down his garden partially because he lost his help in me and partly because he was managing it alone. To make his life easier, he decided to invent a garden plow that attaches to the back of a riding lawn mower.

This idea was not new. Sears had a garden plow you could buy and hook to your lawn mower, and now you can get a similar device from several places. Daddy had bought one and used it for a while. He didn't like it because it kept bouncing up out of the dirt. He got frustrated and decided to design a better one.

So in 1996, after several months of designing and testing, he patented a tilling plow for garden and lawn tractors. It accomplished what he was trying to do. He designed a plow that wouldn't bounce out of the dirt. There was a metal lever on the front of the plow that you would press down, and Dad designed a locking mechanism that kept the lever locked, hence securing the plow in the dirt until you decided to release it. It worked great.

He was excited about his new invention and couldn't wait to contact Sears so he could tell them that he'd invented a better plow. He called Sears, Lowes, Home Depot, and the John Deere Company. He tried for more than a year to get a company who would buy it from him in order to manufacture and sell the plow. He wasn't set up to build it; he just wanted to collect royalties on sales. He never got any interest from the companies.

"Oh, well," he said. "Let's keep plugging away. Next."

U.S. Patent   Mar. 19, 1996   Sheet 3 of 3   **Des. 368,101**

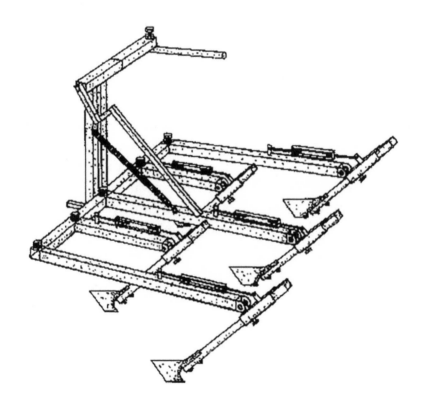

Chapter 7

The Claw Hammer and Cracking Nuts

Daddy's next invention was redesigning the claw hammer.

When he was talking to me about this, I said, "What can you do to improve a hammer?"

I thought maybe that he was going to redesign the head to make it bigger or straightening the angle of the claw. I had no idea what he was up to.

One day he called me and said he wanted me to come over, that he wanted to show me a new claw hammer design he was working on. I went to his shop, and sure enough, he had modified the head of the claw hammer. To my surprise, he didn't make the head bigger, or straighten the angle of the claw. Instead, he welded another claw on the side of the hammerhead to improve the angle of the leverage when you pulled out a nail that you had bent or mistakenly put in the wrong place. It was the weirdest thing I had seen on a hammer. Sure enough, the attachment on the side of the hammerhead worked better than the claw mechanism currently on the back of the hammerhead.

Dad contacted a few different companies such as Lowe's and Home Depot. They weren't interested. Keep in mind, Daddy came up with this idea back in the 1990s. Nearly two decades later, I was shopping at Lowe's, and I came across a claw hammer with the attachment of a side claw similar to what

Daddy had designed. How about that? This makes me wonder, what if?

But it's like what Dad said, let's keep trying.

A year later, after the claw hammer modification, the family had gathered at our parents for the usual Thanksgiving feast. When I walked in, Dad was sitting at the kitchen table cracking open pecans with a foreign object.

"What is that?" I asked.

He said, "It's a nutcracker."

"Not like one I've ever seen," I said.

Daddy chuckled and said, "That's because I have invented the world's most efficient nutcracker, and there's nothing out there like it."

I said, "Please explain."

"Well, it's a redesign on the traditional nutcracker, but it's better simply because it will crack all types of nuts such as Brazil nuts, pecans, black walnuts with superior ease of use. The design of the top plate, which joins the two handles together, is used in conjunction with the offset of the length of the two handles to maximize the ease of cracking the nut and to minimize tension on the handles. The top bolt is used to screw in or out to firmly hold the different-size nuts in place while you squeeze the two handles together in order to crack the shell. The bottom bolt is used to put a stop on squeezing the two handles to close together in order to protect your fingers from being mashed, and the bottom bolt is also used to finish cracking small portions of the shell that was cracked initially by the impact of the top bolt. The sizes of the bolts are one-fourth of an inch. You can use up to five-sixteenth-of-an-inch bolts if desired. Both bolts can be screwed or adjusted in or out to meet customer needs."

After that explanation, I said, "Dad, pass the turkey.'"

We all liked it so much that he showed his nutcracker to various people in the community and at different hardware stores. They thought it was a good idea. He never contacted any companies about it.

RANDY EUBANKS

DAD'S CLAW HAMMER

NUT CRACKER

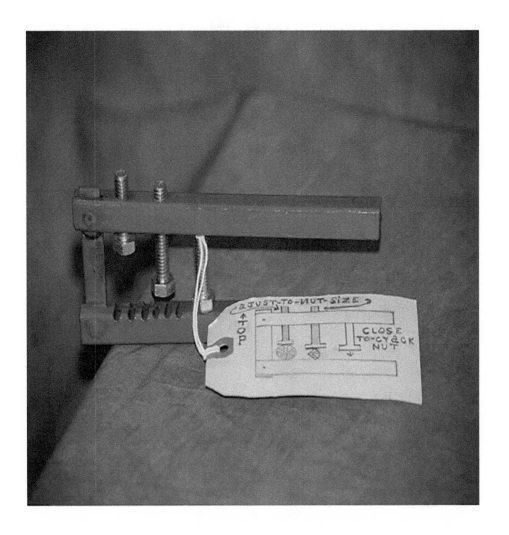

Chapter 8

The Easy Mower

In 1998, my dad started to work on a promising idea that would consume his time and carry us on an exciting adventure over the next fifteen years. His idea became reality in 2001 when he patented the crown prince of all his inventions. We called it the easy mower. A few years later we coined the phrase, "It was so easy to push that even an eighty-year-old World War II veteran can push it with ease."

After three years of thinking and designing, my dad came up with a push lawn mower that anyone could steer with ease. Watching him using the easy mower was like watching a child who had mastered the ability of driving their new battery-powered Jeep. He was a master of maneuvering the mower around bushes and other objects.

The easy mower works like this: to steer, the operator would twist or turn the handle like they were steering a bicycle, and as a result of twisting or turning the handle left or right, the body of the mower would glide sideways, which in turn helped you to mow closer to bushes and other objects.

It was poetry in motion watching my dad push the mower. His goal was to design a mower that would make it fun to mow grass and also eliminate the use of a weed eater for the average homeowner. He didn't like to use a weed eater because they were aggravating to start and he felt that at his age, he and other WWII veterans needed to have devices to make their lives easier.

He was excited about his latest invention, and he was eager to start showing it to different companies. He called and filled out paperwork to submit to the John Deere Company, Troy-Bilt Company, Murray Company, Sears, and Black & Decker. Over the next several months, he corresponded back and forth with these companies. In the end, they all thought it was a good idea, but they said they were afraid to take a chance on spending the money at this point because of the economy. It was another "Next" situation, we thought.

Finally, in the fall of 2000, a company called Country Home Products was interested in looking at it. Daddy shipped the lawn mower to a gentleman named Ric Wheeler. Ric was in charge of new product development. They kept it for a few months. They researched the market potential. Ric was very interested in it personally. He told Daddy that this was a clever invention, and he thought there was a huge market for it. In the end, in opposition to Ric's assessment on the lawn mower, Country Home Products decided not to pursue developing and producing the easy mower. Ric told Daddy off the record that the company was making a mistake. Their excuse was the economy.

Daddy kept calling other companies but to no avail. A few years passed by, and finally Daddy got a break. One morning after his daily walk, he sat down in his living room with his cup of coffee and newspaper. He opened the paper and saw an advertisement soliciting inventors to present their product for a regional contest in Tampa, Florida, for the opportunity to appear on the *American Inventor* show in hopes of winning one million dollars and having your product manufactured by a national company.

Daddy called me up and asked my opinion on entering the contest. I told him we should go for it. In the meantime, I had gotten out of the painting and remodeling business. I was now in the used-car and self-storage business. Daddy got the blessings and support from Mama and my brother and sister and was ready to take another chance. So the journey began. What a great adventure it turned out to be.

COUNTRY HOME PRODUCTS®
75 Meigs Road, P.O. Box 25, Vergennes, VT 05491
Phone: (802)877-1200 Fax: (802)877-1214
Web: countryhomeproducts.com
E-mail: rwheeler@countryhomeproducts.com

Memo

To:	Furney Ewbanks	From:	Ric Wheeler
Fax:		Date:	May 1, 2001
Phone:		Phone:	802-877-1200 x-1120
Re:	Swivel/slide wheel prototypes	Pages:	1

☐ Urgent   ☐ For Review   ☐ Please Comment   ☐ Please Reply   ☐ Please Recycle

Dear Furney:

Thank you for sending the sample trimmer and mower with your very unique slide/swivel wheel. After review, it was determined that we will not be able to explore the development and manufacturing of this idea at this time. We thought the idea was very clever and if you find someone else to develop and produce this machine, we would be interested in talking with them. Of course there are many considerations to be taken into account before a final determination is made to carry a product.

Sincerely,

Ric Wheeler
Country Home Products, Inc.

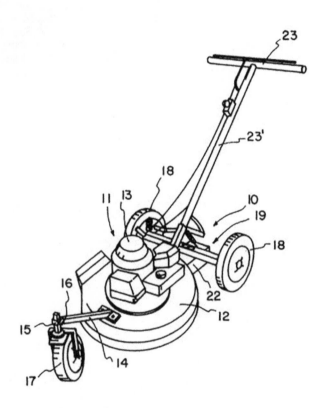

FIG. I

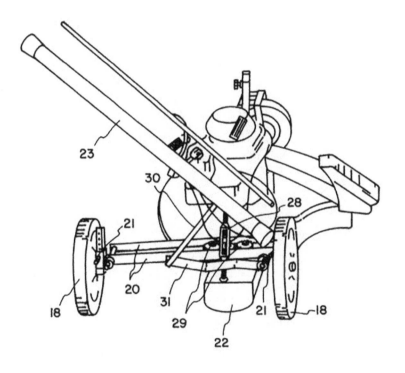

FIG. 3

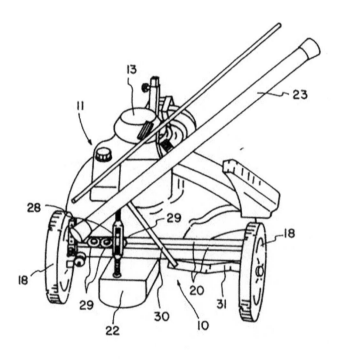

FIG. 4

Chapter 9

Our Journey Begins

Thursday, April 19, 2007.

In preparation for our trip to Tampa, Florida, I packed an adjustable wrench, hammer, jack, and other tools we thought we might need for our demo of the easy mower. Daddy arrived at my office around 11:00 a.m. He told me that he had $1,100 cash with him plus his debit card, something he'd never had before. He offered to pay me to go with him since I wouldn't be at the office selling vehicles.

This is the kind of man he is. He is always thinking about others, and he believes in paying people for services rendered.

I declined and asked him just to furnish all my expenses on the trip. I told him that I was going to eat high on the hog. I did.

We left the office, and I kissed Angela goodbye. Daddy drove a blazer that I had on the car lot and followed me. I drove a Mercury Cougar that we were going to drop off at Aycock Auto Auction on our way to Florida. We stopped in Jacksonville at the bank. It was a funny sight seeing my daddy using a debit card for the first time. My dad and modern technology do not mix. In fact, he has never owned or wanted to own a computer. Using this card for the first time in an ATM machine was quite an experience for him. Good for him I was there to guide him through this process. We left the bank and went to Burger King. Daddy had to have a snack to hold him over until we ate lunch.

We left Jacksonville, North Carolina, and two hours later we were at the auction. As I was driving, I kept thinking about our trip. I pondered what this meant to my father. I wanted him to enjoy every moment of this journey. Unbeknownst to me at this point, my daddy has never been further south than Myrtle Beach, South Carolina. Late one night years later, Daddy admitted something about that trip to Tampa. As the sun was going down over the fields in front of his house, he told me that was the first time he'd been south of Myrtle Beach and that trip meant a lot to him. As I sat on the porch swing with him, I pondered what he had just said and took a sip of my iced tea and replied, "It meant a lot to me also, Dad."

I made up my mind that I was going to enjoy every moment of this trip with my dad. My dad and I were going to spend quality time together.

We spent six memorable days together. I dropped the Mercury Cougar off at the auction. I got in our SUV, a Chevrolet Blazer, with my dad and took over the driving duties, which I never relinquished during the whole trip. That's a good thing because my dad would have gotten us lost. Besides, his job wasn't driving; his job was to present his easy mower in front of the judges in Tampa and come home a winner. We practiced his pitch on the way there. He kept repeating what I told him to say in front of the judges. "The easy mower is so easy to push, that even an eighty-year-old World War II veteran like myself can push it with ease." He repeated this line over and over in the SUV. I must say, he accomplished that task in style. He had a great invention, and he charmed everyone with his style and demeanor.

I will tell you more about this later.

Back to our trip. As we left the auction, I realized we had no need of a radio. He ended up talking nonstop all the way there and all the way back. He told me WWII stories such as how his job was to set up security fences in Berlin and to help feed the families of German widows and their children. He said the American soldiers treated them kindly. Dad was in training camp when Hitler surrendered. When he got to Germany, his job was basically police patrol. My dad was single at the time. This was years before he met my mother. He had brought back from Germany a picture from WWII which was taken of him and this pretty German girl. He didn't bring the picture on the trip. He just mentioned it to me in conversation. I had seen the picture before at his house. Mama didn't seem to mind he still had the picture. I laughed and said, "That German girl could have been my mama." I like to talk a lot myself, but I didn't mind him doing most of the talking; I was soaking up every word he said, enjoying the moment.

I received some very valuable information on World War II such as how politics was involved in which the Americans stepped back and let Russia take Berlin. Dad said it was all politics. He said, "They allowed it because Germany had humiliated Russia in marching over their country, so now it was payback for Russia."

I learned a lot about Dad's family and my ancestors. For example, he told me how great of a businessman my granddaddy was. He also said that Granddaddy was selfish and looked after Granddaddy. He stated, "Granddaddy was only four feet and eleven inches tall. He didn't take no junk. If he loved you, he would give you the shirt off of his back. If he didn't like you, get out of his way."

Some of the information was a review, and some of it was new stuff. My dad has a tendency to repeat himself at times. He believes in small details. It takes him thirty minutes to tell a five-minute story as per my mother. That's okay. I enjoy listening to his stories. He told me the story again of him growing up and how his daddy, my granddaddy, got along with his brothers. My granddaddy was the most productive male sibling in his family according to my dad. Daddy said, "One morning at breakfast, my uncle George came up to my house drunk. I was just a little boy, but I remember like it was yesterday. My uncle was cussing, and Daddy got tired of hearing it. Your granddaddy didn't say a word. He got up from his chair at the breakfast table, went over to the woodstove, and picked up a piece of wood. If it hadn't been for my brother, your uncle Gordon, your granddaddy would have beat Uncle George to death with that piece of wood." I can't tell you how many times Daddy told me that story over the years. The bottom line is "my granddaddy don't take no junk."

We stopped to eat at the Texas Steak House in Smithfield, North Carolina. After I ordered my lunch, it was quite obvious to Dad that I was going to eat high on the hog, or in this case, high on the cow. The term "high on the hog" means that I was going to eat in style. I ordered the biggest and most expensive steak on the menu, and I ate every bite of it. Daddy ordered a small steak, and he didn't finish it. The hamburger that he ate back at Burger King curbed his appetite. He said afterward that if this was a future sign of my eating habits during this trip, he would have been financially better off to pay me and let me furnish my own food.

He laughed and picked on me the whole trip about my eating, but he enjoyed every dollar that he spent on me. As we were riding and talking, I didn't quiz Daddy on some of the questions that the judges might ask him about the easy mower and his other inventions. I wanted him to be relaxed and not to be worried about rehearsing what he was going to say. I told him, "Just remember to tell them, the easy mower is so easy to push, that even an eighty-year-old World War II veteran like myself can push it with ease." That was the only line I wanted him to rehearse. I wanted him to be himself. I told Dad, "If they ask you about your life, by all means, don't tell them that your daddy almost killed your uncle George with a piece of wood. If so, the judges might think we have a crazy family and the apple doesn't fall far from the tree. The judges might ask themselves, is this eighty-year-old man going to attack us if we don't vote his invention as the winner?" Daddy laughed and said, "They don't have to worry about me attacking anybody."

We took our time driving. I averaged between seventy-five to eighty-five miles per hour. We stopped every hour or so and bought snacks and sodas, fuel periodically. We continued the drive and enjoyed the moment. I enjoyed our time together so much that I wanted time to stand still. The reason that I wanted time to stand still was because it was a rarity when a father and his adult son can get away from the daily grinds of every-day life and enjoy a few moments together. I told Dad that in the future, "we needed to get away more often." I wanted Dad and I to enjoy every moment and detail of this trip. We drove until approximately 8:00 p.m. when we stopped in Savannah, Georgia, and got a room at the Fairfield Inn.

We checked in and brought our luggage to the room. We called the family and told them where we were spending the night. After we freshened up, we drove a couple of miles to the Cracker Barrel restaurant. We ate dinner and drove back to the motel. Daddy went to bed. I stayed up and watched some TV but soon dozed off. I woke up Friday morning around 5:30 a.m. at the sound of my dad getting dressed in the bathroom. I didn't know if he was taking a shower or what. We had dis-cussed the night before that he was going to go walking in the morning and I was going running.

Come to find out Dad was in the bathroom taking what I call a birdbath. He washed his face, armpits, and his butt. I hate to even think about what this looks like. Does he stand at the sink, get butt naked, or what? I don't know and I don't care to think about it. I do know this: he didn't take a shower the whole time we were gone. He said that he didn't stink. The fact is I never smelled him. Prior to 1969, before we built our new home, he had bathed for years without a shower. He said that he didn't like to take a shower away from home.

He got dressed, put on his long pants, shirt, and a light coat. I jumped out of bed, put on gym shorts, muscle shirt, and running shoes. We went outside in the dark. He started walking and I took off running. It gave me great joy as I lapped him twice. I was soon humbled when I thought about the age difference between eighty years old and forty-eight. Don't be fooled. He is in great shape for an eighty-year-old man. He can outwalk most people half his age.

Thirty minutes later, we came back to the room. I took a shower and dressed. Daddy sat on the bed, looked at the newspaper, and he waited for me. We left the motel and went next door to eat breakfast at the Waffle House. I had steak, eggs, and pancakes. Dad ate sausage and eggs. We left the restaurant around 8:00 a.m. and took off toward Tampa.

It was a great drive. We drove and talked about the upcoming audition. We had no idea how many inventors would be there. We anticipated a big crowd. Dad and I were excited about the chance to possibly meet George Foreman. He was one of the judges. We had followed his professional boxing career back when George was younger. He himself was also quite an entrepreneur. I enjoyed using the George Foreman Grill. He would be the first famous person that we ever met.

We stopped, got gas and snacks. We were so excited about what might happen coming up in Tampa that we skipped lunch.

Here is what might happen. We could win! If my dad won the *American Inventor* contest, then all his past disappointments dealing with other companies would be forgotten. This victory would make his many hours of hard work in his shop designing his numerous inventions over the years worth the effort. That possibility got us excited.

We drove, and in no time, it seemed like we were at our hotel room in Tampa. We had driven all the way to our first destination, the Sailport Resort Waterfront Suites, without getting lost. We arrived at the beautiful resort on Tampa Bay at 2:00 p.m. The water and scenery was breathtaking. The water was so clear that you could see the bottom. The beautiful palm trees blowing in the wind was something my dad had never seen. The grass looked like green carpet and so neatly trimmed. Dad said with excitement, "They need my easy mower." What a relaxing place. It looked like a tropical paradise, and the sound of the ocean waves made you want to take a nap. My dad said, "No wonder people come to places like this to vacation." On top of that, we were less than one-half of a mile from the Grand Hyatt where the auditions would be taking place on Saturday.

We went to the office and checked in where we met Charles Cabrera, one of the desk managers. He has a son living in Boone, North Carolina, attending Appalachian State University. Dad and I talked with Charles numerous times during our stay.

Our room, suite 255, had a kitchen, living room, and hide-a-bed. This is where I slept; Dad slept in the bedroom down the hallway. The living room had sliding glass doors leading out to a porch balcony. From the balcony, we had a picturesque view of the swimming pool and beyond that, Tampa Bay. The water was beautiful. The surrounding buildings, grass, and trees were a pleasure to gaze upon. I called Angela and told her she did a great job of picking out a place for Daddy and me to stay. We relaxed for a little while in our room.

Since it was 3:30 p.m. and we hadn't eaten since breakfast, we drove around the block and ate at a waterfront restaurant. I had grilled catfish. It was the best catfish that I have ever eaten. Daddy got fried shrimp. We ate outside the restaurant under a covered porch overlooking the water. We relaxed and enjoyed our meal as the breeze cooled us off under the shade of the porch. We took our time, eating and chatting for an hour or so. We finished our meal and took the short drive to the Hyatt where the main event was to take place on Saturday.

This place was huge. We drove and parked on the first level of the parking deck, skipping valet parking. We walked into the lobby and found one of the attendants, who was wearing a dark blue sports coat and a name tag. We asked him about the *American Inventor* show auditions. He told us that we were at the right place. I asked him, "How would the process work tomorrow?" He replied, "There would be signs in the morning directing contestants where to line up." Dad asked the attendant, "Have you ever met George Foreman?" He said, "No."

I told Dad, "They sure don't make hotels like this back home." Dad was just standing there in the middle of the lobby gazing up at the marble columns. There were plants everywhere inside the lobby. He marveled and asked me, "How do they water the plants on top of those marble columns?" I smiled and said, "The plants are artificial." We walked around a few minutes and then drove off. We were now familiar with the territory, which put us at ease. We left with a good feeling since we had found the right place and knew where to be the next day. This helped to relieve some anxiety. We made up our minds to be there early. We left the Hyatt and headed toward the mall to buy Daddy a cap and to look around at the scenery. Dad had left his cap back home, and he needed the cap to shade his sensitive skin. Charles, our buddy, had given us directions to the mall before we had left the room, and after a short drive, we walked through the rear door at JC Penney's and walked through the mall.

As we were walking through the food court, I noticed a kiosk in the middle of the floor with an ice cream sign on it. I wanted an ice cream, so we stopped and talked with the lady there. Come to find out, she and her husband owned two of these businesses and he was at a different mall across the city running another kiosk. I ordered a $5.95 banana split, and Daddy ordered a small ice cream cone. Since Daddy was footing the bill, I didn't mind him paying that price to satisfy my sweet tooth. If I had been buying, I would have ordered a cheap small ice cream cone also. We sat down at one of the tables in the food court and feasted. We finished and asked the lady where we could buy some snacks. She directed us to a Walgreens store outside the mall and across the street. We thanked her and proceeded down the mall on our cap hunt.

We stopped at one of the sporting goods stores and found him a plain brown baseball cap. The clerk had lived in North Carolina. He told us that he was familiar with Camp Lejeune and Jacksonville, North Carolina. His family lived in the mountains. The reason we found out where he lived at was because my daddy asked him where he was from. If we had kept on talking, I feel confident Daddy would somehow discover that we were some of his kinfolk. Needless to say, it took twenty minutes to buy a ten-dollar cap. I finally got Daddy away from the clerk, and we proceeded through the mall and out the front entrance in pursuit of Walgreens.

Walgreens was great and I went crazy. Daddy carried the basket, and I filled it up with goodies. I put in Snicker bars, potato chips, cashews, peanuts, peanut butter crackers, and M&Ms. I spent twenty-six dollars of Daddy's money on snacks. We agreed we weren't going to eat supper that night since we ate a late lunch and had so many snacks. Those snacks weren't just dinner; we needed them to tie us over until the next day.

It was a long way from Walgreens back to our vehicle. We are both fast walkers, so it didn't seem that long before we were at the car; a short drive later and we were back at our room. It was a little after 7:00 p.m., and Dad was tired, so we talked a few minutes, while I put the snacks and sodas away. Soon Daddy said that he was going to bed. He was tired, and we had a long day ahead of us. It was around 7:30 p.m. and I wasn't sleepy, so I told Daddy that I was going for a walk. I went down to the restaurant we had eaten at earlier. I went to the bar, ordered a sweet tea, and listened to the band play a few minutes. As I was listening to the music, I took out a piece of paper and wrote down what to bring with us tomorrow for the audition. The filled-out applications and the DVD along with the easy mower were all we needed. I finished my drink and walked back to my room as the sun was setting. I pulled out my hide-a-bed and watched TV until midnight.

Chapter 10

It's Showtime

The next thing I remember was Daddy's loud mouth at 3:30 a.m. telling me that he was through in the bathroom. Lucky for me I had filled up the coffeepot the night before and had the timer set for 3:45 a.m. The attendant we had met the day before said to be at the Hyatt by 6:00 a.m. Daddy had already taken his birdbath and was dressed. I showered, dressed, and poured us a cup of coffee. I sure needed that cup. We were out the door at 4:15 a.m. Thirty minutes later, we were one of the first ten inventors standing in line at the Hyatt. To people who know my father, that is not a surprise. He is always early. He does not tolerate tardiness.

The other nine contestants started forming a line outside of the hotel in front of what looked like a big revival tent. We waited in line around forty-five minutes, then we were directed around the back of the Hyatt to form a new or the official line behind the hotel. The few inventors who had spent the night at the Hyatt would have the privilege of being the first ones in the official line. This was a fringe benefit of spending the night in the hotel. Those of us waiting on the front side of the hotel by the tent would fall in line behind them when the time came to march toward the back of the hotel. The rest of us were in what I called the unofficial line in front of the hotel. It was unofficial to me because the line that counted was the one in the back of the hotel. Later on, the unofficial line in front would merge with the official line behind the building, forming one line.

The unofficial line started to grow. With all these inventions, we wondered would our easy mower get noticed. To say the least, this made us nervous. I said to myself, "I hope we haven't wasted our time." While we were in line, Daddy and I talked to some of the other inventors. There were inventors from all over the country. They had all kinds of gadgets such as redesigned coffeepots, commercial cake cutter, exercise equipment, doggy barf bag, wrap-a-way cabinet / gift wrapper (installable wrap organizer that keeps multiple types of wrap—aluminum, saran, etc.). One inventor told us about a unique invention that he saw back in his home state which was called the guardian angel: water extinguisher system that puts out Christmas tree fires.

We left the mower in the back of the blazer because we wanted to find out where we would be lining up before we revealed the easy mower. Daddy kept my place in line while I went to the vehicle to get the mower. It was still dark when I got the easy mower and pushed it down the parking deck onto the cobblestoned sidewalk where Daddy was. Almost immediately the people in line started noticing it and asking us questions about the mower. One contestant asked us, "How long did it take to design the mower?" Another one asked, "How many have you sold?" Daddy responded, "Zero, that is the reason we are here. We want to get a company to sell them for us." We met some interesting people, and we started questioning each other back and forth about the different inventions. The lady who invented the doggy barf bag brought her poodle dog with her. She was so impressed with our mower after seeing Daddy playing with it that she said, "I might as well carry my doggy bag and poodle back to Georgia." You have to imagine seeing my daddy while he was standing in line demonstrating his mower by pushing it back and forth and steering it around in circles. It was quite amusing watching him show off his invention. He acted like a little boy at Christmas opening his brand-new Tonka truck and pushing it around the living room. I asked the gentleman who invented the wrap-a-way cabinet / gift wrapper, "What gave you that idea?" He said, "I got tired of my disorganized pantry. Plus, he said, "I love to build cabinets."

Dad and I noticed that a lot of the inventions were covered up. They were in boxes, bags, wrapping paper, and some were wrapped with blankets. There was one invention covered by a Pittsburgh Steelers blanket that got my attention because I am a huge Steelers fan. I asked the gentleman, "What's under that blanket?" He said, "It's a secret." He wouldn't tell me or show me his invention. I assumed this secrecy was a result of the inventions not being patented and the inventors' fears that someone would steal their ideas.

We met a middle-aged man named Bobby in line behind us. He was retired from the South Carolina school system where he had worked in a school cafeteria. He was currently employed by a contractor who transported food to the different schools in the county where he lived. Bobby designed a commercial cake cutter and had previously auditioned for the *American Inventor* show. In his other audition, he made it past the first two rounds, and the judges told him that they liked his idea, but before he appeared in front of the final judges he needed a working prototype. He only had drawings with him in New York, so he went back to his home and made a prototype. He was here in Tampa to show the judges his working model.

That reminded me of the purpose of our trip. ABC was about to start airing its second season of *American Inventor*, a reality competition show, the first six episodes of which were going to take place on the road. Judges would pick finalists from the six audition cities—Los Angeles, San Francisco, Chicago, New York, Houston, and Tampa Bay—like they do on *American Idol.* The judges were Sara Blakely, George Foreman, Pat Croce, and Peter Jones. The winner from each city receives a fifty-thousand-dollar check to further develop and put finishing touches on their product. The seventh and final show, a two-hour episode, would focus on the six finalists as they prepare their prototypes and presentation to the judges. The judges would pick the three finalists, and viewers would vote for their favorite invention. The winner gets one million dollars and will have the opportunity to market their product worldwide. This was why we were doing this.

At this time, one of the producers told all of us in line to follow him. Unbeknownst to me, the excitement was about to begin.

Chapter 11

It Fell Apart at the Wrong Time

It could have been a disaster.

Here's what happened.

The line moved from the tent in front of the hotel to the back of the Hyatt at a fast pace. Daddy was speed walking ahead of me like he was going to a fire. All the people were rushing in anticipation of finally seeing the judges. I took off pushing the easy mower quickly along the cobblestoned sidewalk. All of a sudden, the rear right side of the mower separated from the main frame. So here I was pushing a mower with most of the weight on the front wheel because the back wheels were no longer functional. I had to pick up the back of the mower by the handle and keep the dangling wheels off the ground. I thought for a moment the whole mower was going to fall apart. The way it was acting I could only imagine that parts were falling off as I was pushing it. I didn't have time to look back and see if any parts had fallen off. If I had stopped, I would have gotten stampeded by what seemed like wild cattle prancing behind me. All of us inventors were moving at a frantic pace.

In the meantime, Daddy was way ahead of me prancing along, not aware of my serious problem. Thank goodness, Bobby was beside me, and I asked him to run ahead and tell Daddy what was going on. I knew that the line would stop moving soon, giving me time to stop and regroup. But whatever happened, I wasn't going to stop and lose my place in line, and neither was Daddy. I was going to get this mower behind the hotel in the official line, even if I had to pick it up and carry it.

On top of this, as I approached the back side of the hotel, I noticed approaching in front of me a set of steps. I said to myself, "How in the world am I going to make it down those steps?" I had to somehow push this broke-down mower down the steps in two different areas. There was a ten-foot drop from the elevation of the ground on the side of the hotel to the elevation of the ground on the back. As I paused and looked at the grim task of pushing this broke-down mower down those steep narrow steps, I said a little prayer to myself and started pushing the mower down the cobblestoned steps, which were only three feet wide. I had to take my time, and I could feel the breath of the person behind me panting on my neck. He must have been thinking, "Why don't this man get out of my way?" I could feel the drops of water forming under my armpits. It was good for the person behind me that I didn't take a birdbath like my dad did that morning. I was nervous and sweating. I could hear the sound of people's shoes banging on the cobblestone behind me as I made it down the first set of steps and then the second set of steps.

Thank God, I was able to get the mower behind the hotel and on the long breezeway where the line had stopped. By this time, Bobby had told Daddy I was having some difficulties with the mower. I reunited with Daddy in the line, and he evaluated the situation. Luckily for us, it was still dark and the doors wouldn't be open for another hour, so there were no cameras on us and the production staff didn't notice us yet.

Daddy immediately knew what the problem was. The bolts and nuts that adjusted the swivel mechanism weren't tight enough and had worked their way loose as I was pushing the mower along the cobblestoned sidewalk. I told Daddy that I had brought an adjustable wrench with us just in case we needed it. Daddy intended on bringing some tools, but he left them in his truck back at my office. I told him to hang right here. I took off running to the parking deck to retrieve the adjustable wrench that was in the Blazer. It seemed like it took forever to go get that wrench and come back. It felt this way because we had a big problem, which was a broke-down mower. I wanted to get it fixed fast before anybody important such as one of the producers of the show saw our easy mower in this condition. As I was turning the corner around the side of the hotel, the line was starting to get long and it wasn't even 6:00 a.m. yet. It seemed like it stretched for a mile. I am exaggerating a little, but there must have been at least 250 people in the line stretching out on the side of the building and in the front of the Hyatt. I got the wrench, and I ran to get in line beside my daddy. He was down on his knees attempting to tighten the bolts with a small pair of pliers that he had borrowed from someone in line. He was relieved to see that I had the adjustable wrench in my hand. He took the wrench, and in a matter of minutes he had the mower back together and as good as new. He said that when he got back home with the mower he was going to put some lock washers on it. Daddy said, "I can't believe I didn't put any lock washers under these nuts. Oh well, I also never figured that someone would be pushing the easy mower down a flight of rough cobblestoned steps either." He laughed and said, "We dodged a bullet." Installing lock washers would eliminate the bolt-loosening problem in the future. As I previously stated, I had originally thought when the mower came apart that some of the pieces had fallen off and possibly gotten lost. I had asked Bobby, "Would you go back and look to see if any parts of the mower were on the ground." Bobby said he would be glad to.

In a few minutes, Bobby came running back and said, "I didn't see anything."

I was so thankful that all it took was an adjustable wrench to fix the problem. I told Daddy I had a new name for the wrench.

"From now on we're calling that wrench by a new name, Daddy," I said. "In your hands you hold the million-dollar wrench.'"

My daddy chuckled and looked at the wrench. "You know what?" he said. "Could be you're right. This wrench might have just made us a million bucks." All of a sudden, our confidence skyrocketed. I said, "We are destined to win this thing." Dad said, "It's a done deal. Just give us our check." We both chuckled.

If I hadn't brought the adjustable wrench, he would have been in trouble. We would have gone home defeated with a broke-down mower. The good news is we were prepared. From this moment on, great circumstances and favor were upon us the rest of that day and the remainder of the trip. It got better, and it got better quick.

In the meantime, we had about an hour to wait in line before they opened up to start the process. A lot of interesting things began to happen.

To start with, we met more interesting people. We met a man named Dave and his young son. Dave was a missionary from Florida. Dave was very secretive about his invention. He had it hidden in a paper box. I hesitated to ask him what was in there. I could only imagine. Could it be the next great video game? Could it be a new toy that will bust all sales records? Whatever it was, his young son was taking in all the surroundings, and he seemed to be enjoying the moment. Dave told us about his recent missionary trip to the remote jungles in Africa. He talked about the danger and persecutions that Christians faced overseas. He stated, "You could and many did lose their lives for professing to be a Christian. We are so blessed, and we take our religious freedom for granted in this country."

We met others who had various inventions, some of which we didn't see because they were covered up.

There was a heating and air contractor named Jeff from Georgia. He had designed some fitting to put on a heat pump to help save energy. I didn't understand what he was talking about, considering he was talking in technical lingo, which was above my pay grade. Jeff was technically smart, but he lacked in the ability to plan properly. He said this, "I spent one thousand dollars and lost three days of work on a wasted trip to Orlando, Florida, a few days ago."

The reason was simple: bad planning on his part. This event was originally scheduled to take place in Orlando on April 10, but it was cancelled. The show posted updates on their web page, but for a few days they didn't reveal the new location. Still, they gave more than a week's notice that the new location would be in Tampa. I can't imagine anyone taking off to Orlando and not knowing for sure if the event was going to end up being there. In my opinion, Jeff didn't make the proper preparations. If he would have kept checking the updates on their web page and or called the toll-free number, he would have saved his one thousand dollars and not lost three days of work.

Suddenly, I noticed out of the corner of my eye a dog rolling in the grass. I looked around, and this gentleman, apparently the dog's owner, was blowing on a slender pencil-looking pipe. As the man blew on the pipe the dog would do different tricks. My curiosity got the best of me. I said, "Sir, excuse me, how is blowing through that pipe making the dog roll over, stand on his back legs, extend his paw to shake your hand, and you not saying a word or no sound coming out of the pipe." He smiled and said, "It's the technology built inside the pipe which puts out different sound waves that only the dog can under-stand." He went on to say, "My invention will revolutionize dog training." That's all he would say about it.

As the dog was rolling in the grass, a woman riding a bicycle with a battery pack on it came cruising by. She started demonstrating her electric bike. I thought to myself, that takes the exercise out of bike riding. She was just sitting there riding on the bike with the battery pack turning the wheels. In the meantime, Jeff was still complaining.

Chapter 12

Preparation Pays Off

After Jeff had finished his rant, one of the crew members of the production team made a loud announcement, asking for a show of hands from the inventors who needed applications to fill out. There was a large number of people who raised their hands. I couldn't believe what I was seeing. You mean to tell me that some of these people who had come slam across this country to stand in line in the early hours of the morning for an opportunity to be the next American inventor and possibly have the chance to make a million dollars on their invention didn't take the time to fill out the application before they arrived?

There were three applications with a total of thirty-three pages. Each had to be filled out in detail, and there had to be copies of your driver's license and birth certificate attached. There were over one hundred pages of fine print in their contract in which we read. How dumb can somebody be? How could anyone be stupid enough to think they had a chance to win and they have waited until the last minute when you are being rushed to fill out the detailed application while standing in line?

These people are surprised when they lose out. They say things like, "So-and-so are lucky." They say, "That's just my bad luck." They create their fate by their lack of preparation and procrastination. I memorized a saying by Earl Nightingale that says, "The definition of luck is when preparedness meets opportunity, and opportunity is always there." Daddy and I had been preparing for this opportunity for a while. In fact, Daddy has been preparing for this opportunity for fifty-one years.

It all started in 1956 when he made his first invention. Remember the story I told you at the beginning when Dad invented a more efficient tobacco harvester clip? I will remind you what Mr. Long said. Mr. Long told Daddy, "Mr. Eubanks, you are two years too late. We are in the process of developing our automatic croppers. Two years sooner on this design, you would have been a rich man. However, I do not want anyone else to have this. I will pay you five hundred for it right now and patent it myself. I will give you a job in the company, send you to school, and give you a percentage on all new inventions and redesigns you come up with." That was the beginning of this process and Dad's preparation for this moment.

He didn't wait until the last minute to fill out an application while standing in line. My dad got "lucky" because he was prepared. Let me share how he was prepared for this opportunity.

Throughout the years, he kept plugging away. He didn't give up when discouragement tried to set in as a result of companies not wanting to build his inventions like the tool holder, garden plow, elevation station for painters, paint can holder, unique-designed claw hammer. He didn't have to stand in line trying to cover up and hide the easy mower. The easy mower was patented, and everything pertaining to its design and structure was paid for. He spent three years of his life designing and redesigning it until he got it right. He obtained the protections on it and had the liberty to show off the easy mower to anyone who wanted to look at it.

This paid off greatly for him at the audition. His invention was one of the most popular ones there, and it seemed like everybody looked at it. Many of the inventors commented that there was no need for them to go any further; Daddy was already the winner as far as they were concerned.

And it was all thanks to his preparation and hard work. Throughout the years he paid for all his inventions and patents as he went along. He worked extra hours in his upholstery shop to accomplish this. He didn't allow his hobby of inventing to take money away from his family. He even consulted with his family to get their blessings and support before he took this trip to Florida.

One Saturday less than a month before the Florida auditions, Daddy; Mama; my sister, Joan; her husband, Pate; my brother, Jacky; his wife, Pat; and I met for breakfast at a Golden Corral in Jacksonville, North Carolina, to discuss Daddy going to Orlando, Florida, to audition for the second season of the *American Inventor* show that would be on ABC later that summer. We talked and decided that I would go with Daddy to Florida.

We discussed flying versus driving. We talked about the cost of going to California in case he won in Florida. We discussed the whole process all the way through. There was the application and lengthy contract, what patent documents we needed and what other paperwork we should take. We discussed that this is a reality show.

I commented, "They would not embarrass an eighty-year-old WWII veteran. That would not be politically correct." Joan said, "I will help Daddy fill out the applications." Jacky asked, "Daddy, if this is what you want to do in your heart, then do it."

We set up a detailed to-do list with time deadlines to make this thing happen. We didn't have much time since the auditions were scheduled to take place in Orlando on Tuesday, April 10, less than a month away.

After breakfast, I invited Joan, Pate, Jacky, and Pat to my house to review the DVD that Tutt Productions made for Daddy. Tutt Productions was a studio in Kinston, North Carolina that filmed commercials for clients. Dad had hired them to make a video for us to present to the judges in Florida.

As we drove up to the house, Angela and my son-in-law Derrick, who was married at that time to our oldest daughter, Brandy, were in the front yard planting flowers in the flower bed. Derrick had skin in this process since Daddy had hired him to put a slick paint job on the easy mower.

I told everyone that "the DVD needed to be edited to fit into the time frame. Plus, we need to take out numerous 'ah's' Daddy had inserted in his grammar." Daddy did the best he could, but he tends to ramble on. He's not a toastmaster by any means. He is all country in his actions and his speaking. By the time we analyzed the DVD, I told the group, "I feel confident we can reduce this ten-minute video down to two minutes after we remove the repeated sentences and all the 'ah's.'" Everybody chuckled and agreed. After all of us reviewed the tape, along with Angela and my son, Randall, we wrote Daddy a new script to read.

I insisted that part of his new script would read, "The mower is so easy to use that even an eighty-year-old World War II veteran like me can use it."

I knew for TV purposes we had to utilize Daddy's assets. For example, an eighty-year-old man in great shape. He is a WWII veteran. He has been trying for fifty-one years to get one of his inventions on the market. We all agreed his story would make for great TV. On top of this, our daddy has a wonderful charm and a great personality; everybody loves him. We wrote a draft of a script for Daddy to learn and read. It was short and to the point. With the new script, his great mower, and his personality, we shared a unanimous opinion that Daddy had a great chance of winning.

On the following Wednesday, I drove to Daddy's house where Daddy, Mama, and I talked a few minutes before we left to drive to Kinston to meet with Clark Tutt.

I told Daddy, "We need to carry the easy mower with us to Florida. I will drive to Florida instead of us flying. We can transport the mower with us in the vehicle." I also suggested, "We will let Derrick fix the welding joints and repaint the mower to make it look like a finished and factory product."

He agreed.

We met Clark Tutt at his office, and Daddy read his new script. Clark was able to insert the new dialogue into the DVD and edit it down to 1:30, under the 2-minute maximum length specified in the application. We left Kinston and went back to Daddy's house, loaded the easy mower into the back of Daddy's truck, and then off to Jacksonville to carry the mower to Derrick so he could paint it.

That Friday, Angela, Joan, and I spent five hours at my office with Daddy and Mama going over the applications. We made blank copies. Joan handwrote a rough draft. She spent a great amount of time on the phone with Daddy's patent attorney getting patent numbers and filing dates for Daddy's numerous inventions.

We coached Daddy on how to answer questions that I had written for him concerning his mower and other inventions he had designed. We were preparing him for questions that the judges might ask him. Pretending to be George Foreman, the first question I asked, "Mr. Eubanks, what inspired you to invent the easy mower?" My dad said, "Ah, um, I didn't have Randy around the house anymore to mow the grass, so I started thinking there are probably thousands and thousands of families across the country who no longer has a Randy to mow their yard. So, I needed to come up with an easier way to mow grass." I couldn't believe he responded like that. I said, "Daddy, you can't answer that way. You better rethink your answer. The judges will laugh you off the stage." Dad said, "Well, that was the inspiring reason to invent a better mower." I said, "Joan, your turn."

My sister, representing Sara Blakely, asked my dad, "May I call you Furney?"

Dad said, "You sure may, sweetheart."

"My question is, do you think a petite lady, like myself, could push your lawn mower with ease?"

My dad said, "Well, honey, if you have a problem pushing this mower, here is my number, I will be right over." My dad just grinned from ear to ear. I said, "Let's call it a day."

Over the course of the next few days, Joan spent hours rewriting the answers on the final draft of the applications, all of which Daddy signed before he left my office on that Friday.

Joan brought me the signed final drafts of the three applications a few days later. I made copies of the originals for my file, and I brought the extra copies with me to Florida in case that the originals got damaged. Joan took a picture of Daddy, and I took a picture of the mower. We attached the pictures to the applications along with a copy of his birth certificate and driver's license.

As Daddy and I got ready to leave for Florida, I packed the easy mower, which we had stored in my garage since Derrick finished repainting it. I packed five copies of the DVD, all the filled-out applications, and other pertinent items for this trip. I even made a smart move by packing the million-dollar wrench.

To top it all off and to add to the preparation of this opportunity, my daddy has lived a clean life. After Saturday's two rounds of judging, we carried another application back to our hotel room to be filled out and brought back with us on Monday. This application was a background questionnaire consisting of 119 questions. These questions were pertaining to what kind of life that my dad has lived that asked questions, such as, "Have you ever been arrested as an adult or minor?" "Do you have any outstanding judgements against you?" "Have you any current or outstanding warrants?" "Have you ever declared bankruptcy?" "Have you ever had a restraining order placed against you?" "Have you ever had any property repossessed to include voluntary repossessions?" "Have you ever been detained by the police as an adult or minor?" The answer to these and many more personal questions was a resounding *no*! I am not sure why they were asking all these personal questions. In fact, there were 119 questions in all. I assumed they were looking for the perfect person. Who knows.

Though it was lengthy, it was a pleasure to fill this out as I was looking over it Sunday afternoon. There are no flaws on his record except maybe one. What a wonderful example my daddy's life has been for his children to model after. My dad has always been a great provider for his family. He was morally pure as far as I knew. The only flaw I ever known him to commit and this was my mama's version of the story. She told me the story of Daddy going on a chilly winter day out to the church house to fix the frozen water pump. This supposedly happened years ago before I was born. My mom said, "Your daddy got cold working on the frozen water pump. So, Daddy goes out to his truck and comes back with a pint of whiskey to keep himself warm. Dad decided to try a sip. The next thing you know, the bottle was empty and your daddy was drunk. When he came home, I made him sleep outside that night." I am not sure how much my mom exaggerated that story, but it happened many years ago. I don't think he ever took another drink again to this day. I am pretty sure God forgave him for getting drunk while fixing the water pump for the church.

As I was filling out that application, I realized that living a clean and respectable life had helped prepare him for this opportunity. I thought and pondered this, and I recommitted to myself that day to live a life that my wife, kids, and future grandkids would be proud of.

Chapter 13

They Gave Us a Number

The staff passed out the applications to the inventors needing them, and suddenly a camera crew came out of the glass doors leading inside the hotel. They started interviewing the inventors. I tried my best to put ourselves in position to be seen by the camera crew, but we just missed them because I was still looking at and pondering the people standing in line filling out the applications. I tried to make up for this by jumping out of line and pushing the mower across the grass at the camera man and acting like it got away from me. I couldn't believe that he didn't notice me since the lawn mower almost hit the back of his leg as he was walking away. I said," Excuse me." He nodded and moved on. He acted like he was in a hurry and took off. I brought the lawn mower back in line, and Dad said, "What was that episode about?" I replied, "I was trying to get noticed." Other contestants ahead of us in line were waving at the camera. Some even held up their inventions as the camera crew passed by. That was the last time that we would miss the camera crew. They opened up the glass doors, and the registration process started. As we got closer to the glass doors, an employee took our completed applications, and we were ushered inside.

The excitement was intense. As we entered the building, we had to empty our pockets for the security guards to check our belongings. Daddy had to give up his pocket knife. We convinced them to let me keep the million-dollar wrench in case we needed it to work on the easy mower. Daddy said, "Do you want me to pull off my shoes too? This is like going through airport security." I replied, "How do you know what airport security is like? When was the last time you've been up in a plane?" I answered for him before he got a chance to open his mouth. "World War II was the last time you were in a plane." He said, "No, don't you remember when they flew the veterans up to the World War II Memorial Museum in Washington, DC, a couple of years ago. That was when they frisked me like they are wanting to do here." The security guard said, "Move on and good luck."

We got through security and waited in a small line in front of the registration desk. Four people sat behind a table to the side of the registration desk; they told us if we needed to show a DVD as part of our demonstration to get in line to the right, so that's what we did.

I picked up two brochures at the side table describing the events for the day. I read one of the brochures while we waited in line. The brochure listed the judges' names and had their pictures on the inside of the trifold. What got me pumped up was the next statement I read in the brochure. "The contestants will compete for a chance to win one million dollars and the opportunity for a company to manufacture and sell the winner's product." That gave me goose bumps. I told Dad, "The winner could be us." Dad smiled and said, "You might be right." The nervous juices were starting to flow. It was soon Daddy's turn to register. The lady at the registration desk talked to us a few minutes. She already had his applications and was looking over them. She said, "Mr. Eubanks, welcome to the contest. I see you are from Trenton, North Carolina. How was the drive up?" she said. I said, "It was great, my dad talked nonstop all the way up." She laughed and said, "Here is your number." Dad said, "Wow, that is a mighty large number." She gave us a number and told us to move forward and a staff member would direct us to a waiting room. Our number was 6016.

We continued moving down the hallway until a staff member directed us to the first room on the left. We thought this was it, but it was only a big open banquet room. It was a bit awkward maneuvering a push lawn mower around the chairs and people. We took our seat and waited for number 6016 to be called.

In the meantime, the other inventors started paying close attention to Daddy's mower. Throughout the day, he was constantly showing people how the mower worked. He would get up and start pushing the mower around the room talking to people. They seemed very interested. I believe they were just as interested in hearing him talk about the easy mower versus the easy mower itself. Daddy is a good talker, and he has this country accent that people love.

Around 10:30 a.m., they called Daddy's name and number, and we went across the hallway into another room that was partitioned off by black curtains. It looked like they had divided and made four rooms out of one big room. I pushed the mower inside the room; the DVD was in my pocket, and Daddy was beside me. There were a man and two women sitting behind a table. There was also a cameraman in the room filming the event. The young man sitting behind the table looked to be in his twenties. He asked all the questions and was the only one of the three who talked. The two women typed on their laptops the whole time.

Daddy introduced us and described how the mower worked and performed a demonstration. Dad said, "You steer the mower around the bushes like you are driving a car. The easy mower is so easy to push, that even an eighty-year-old

World War II veteran can do it." I almost urinated in my pants with excitement. He memorized the famous line I told him to say, and he delivered it with elegance. I was so proud of him. The young man asked Dad a few questions about the mower. I gave the cameraman the DVD. He played it. I noticed as he was watching the DVD that he looked at the two ladies typing on the laptops and nodded to them with approval.

The young man smiled at us and said, "Congratulations, you've made it through the first round."

We strolled out the room with excitement. A staff member told us to go back in the big waiting room until it was time to go to the next interview, which was round two. When we went back into the big waiting room, they directed us to the opposite end of the room where we were seated earlier. A couple of people in the room asked how did it go. Dad said, "All is well. We are off to round two." "Congratulations," they said while we pulled up a couple of chairs.

We talked to each other about what had just occurred. I said, "Wow! I am glad to be moving on to round two." Dad responded, "Me too." Dad asked, "What do you think those two ladies were typing on their laptops?" I blurted out, "I don't know. But I know this, we are moving on to round two." "Hallelujah!" my daddy shouted.

I told Daddy that I was going to call Angela. Here is how the conversation went with her. "Hello, honey. Guess what?" She said, "What?" I quickly replied, "They said our invention sucked, go back home. Not! Just kidding. We are moving on to round two." She said, "Congratulations." Then she started drilling me on questions such as, "Who was in the room with you two?" "Were you nervous?" "Did you meet anyone famous?" I told her not yet. However, the way things were going, soon Daddy would be a star. I said, "I need to call Joan right quick before they call us into the next interview." Angela wished us luck. I called Joan and filled her in. Joan couldn't contain herself. She tended to get emotional. Joan said, "When are you going to meet George Foreman? Tell Sara Blakely I said hello." I said, "Calm down and hold your horses. That was just round one." I have got to call Jacky right quick before we were called for the next round. My brother, Jacky, is more on the reserved side than my sister. I called and said, "Hi, Jacky, Daddy and I are still in the game." He said in a quiet voice, "That's great man. What does Daddy think?" I shouted, "What does Daddy think? He is about to pee in his pants with excitement! There is your update, Jacky, I have got to go, bye!" I got everybody updated. I told Joan to call Mama.

Daddy and I were in the waiting room from around 11:15 a.m. until 2:00 p.m. We were getting hungry, but if we left we were afraid that we would miss our second interview. Besides, we were too excited to eat. We decided that we would eat a big dinner when the day was over. The time passed quickly. Time flies when you are having fun. It was fun just being in this atmosphere of anticipation. We were anticipating that we wanted to win. We met more inventors. I will have to be honest. I wasn't really paying attention to their inventions. I was so focused on Daddy and his easy mower. I admit, I was selfish. I don't even remember their names or their inventions. I wanted him to win this contest so much that I was totally focused on us. He deserves it. For some reason, people just flocked to him and his invention. The other inventors just loved how the mower steered and the body of the mower swiveled just by turning the steering handle. Plus, it was funny seeing my eighty-year-old dad pushing that mower around chairs in that large room pretending the chairs were small bushes that he was mowing around. Don't worry, he never cranked the mower inside of the room.

During this time, a man came up and introduced himself as a photographer with the *Tampa Tribune*. He started taking pictures of the easy mower along with pictures of Dad and me. He asked us a few questions about the mower and exited the room. In just a few minutes, he came back with another person who introduced himself as Mike Wells, staff writer for the *Tampa Tribune*. He did an extensive interview with Dad and me. After he left, we looked at each other and smiled. I said, "We have a good chance, Dad, of winning this." We both felt great and were on cloud nine.

The other inventors had looked on with amazement as we were being interviewed. Daddy told Mike about all his inventions, starting with improving a tobacco-holding clip on a tobacco harvester back in 1956 to his present-day invention of the easy mower. Mike said, "The write-up would be in Sunday's newspaper." Dad replied, "I look forward to reading it." He shook his hand, and they left the room. We couldn't wait to see Sunday's paper. In the meantime, we had an upcoming second-round interview to attend.

While we were still in the waiting room, a lady from the production crew came by and interviewed us. Daddy is such a charmer. He is the type of guy that you want to carry home with you to meet your mama. He loves everybody, and he makes people feel good because he comes across as a caring person. His charming personality stole the show. He and his product attracted more attention by far than the rest of the inventions. A production staff employee came and got us at two on the dot. She escorted us to the hallway, where we waited until it was our time to go in. We were there for just a few minutes, then it was our turn.

We went through the doorway, and instead of going to the far room on the right like last time, we went to the far room on the left. The room was basically set up like the first one we were in that morning, except there was a man in his late thirties sitting behind a table. He sat between two women, and he did all the talking while the other two typed on their laptops and never looked up. There were cameras around us and in the ceiling but no cameraman in the room this time.

The man asked us questions.

He quizzed Dad on his World War II experiences in great detail. He asked, "What was your MOS in the Army?" Dad replied, "Artillery." He also asked Daddy, "Where was your duty station?" Dad replied, "Germany." He continued and asked, "How did you like being stationed in Germany?" Daddy said, "The weather was ugly. However, the women were pretty." The guy couldn't help but laugh. He asked about the mower, and Daddy demonstrated how it worked.

I gave the man the DVD. He played it.

He told us, "I hope that you have some extra clothes packed, because you will be back on Monday to appear before the real judges at the A La Carte Event Pavilion."

To say the least, Daddy and I were excited. We came out of the room pumped up. We hugged each other and gave one another high fives. I cried out, "That's what I am talking about. Yes, we did it."

We waited in the hallway to take the next step: meeting a man named Chris Licato. He was a nice guy. He liked us. We could tell this by how he was interacting with us. We just hit it off. Chris liked us so much that he had one of his friends take a picture of him standing with us. He talked with us a few minutes and wrote down some information on Daddy. He gave us directions to A La Carte Event Pavilion. This is the place where we'd go on Monday to appear before the real judges: Sara Blakely, George Foreman, Pat Croce, and Peter Jones.

We had a chance while we were waiting to see Chris to talk to our air conditioner contractor friend Jeff. Jeff was excited because he had made it to the finals. He would be over at the A La Carte Event Pavilion on Monday to pitch his invention to the judges too.

We talked to more inventors in the hallway.

We talked to a couple of inventors who had invented a telescoping pole with a gizmo on the end of it in which you could change smoke detectors in tall ceilings without getting on a ladder. Dad liked that invention because it was like the tool holder he had invented a few years earlier. Daddy's tool holder was screwed on the end of a pole where this gizmo was permanently attached to their telescoping pole. They were on standby for Monday. They were maybes. Apparently the panel hadn't decided whether these inventors were moving on or not. They didn't make it. We never saw them again.

After we finished talking to Chris, he gave us a 119-item questionnaire for us to fill out over the weekend and bring back on Monday.

In just a few minutes Michael, a member of the staff, came and got us. He led us to the registration desk where we started this morning in order to film us reenacting the registration process. When we got to the desk, other contestants were still in line registering. The line was very long, so Michael changed his mind and he took us out on the lawn behind the Hyatt for our interview. There was plenty of green grass to demonstrate the easy mower.

In just a few minutes, the camera crew came outside where Daddy and I were standing. This young Italian girl interviewed Daddy. She was smoking hot. She had long dark black hair and a beautiful tan. My dad said, "You sure are pretty." She said, "Thank you, Mr. Eubanks." Daddy said, "You can call me Furney." "You are a cutie," she said. She immediately fell in love with him and said, "Furney, I am going to carry you back to California with me." Daddy laughed and replied, "My wife might not like that." I immediately told Daddy, "What goes on in Tampa stays in Tampa."

It was fun watching Daddy being interviewed. He ate it up. He was blushing all over. I have never seen him this excited. I thought that he was going to jump out of his pants. It was a funny sight watching him pretend to mow grass around the bushes. He would steer that mower, weaving in and around the bushes like it was a work of art pushing a lawn mower. I can say that he gave them a show. He's a natural in front of the camera.

They took pictures of us. They filmed him pushing the mower in the grass. The strange thing was they never asked him to crank the easy mower. The only thing I could figure was they didn't want the background noise of an engine running. Who knows for sure?

After they finished interviewing Daddy, they inserted us into the line with all the other contestants who were waiting to register for this event. We had gone through their process hours before. We felt their nervousness and anxiety. They put us into the line in order to film us standing there. They were back-tracking, shooting our "registration" process because we were one of the finalists to be interviewed before the real judges this upcoming Monday.

We were excited to say the least. It was around 4:00 p.m., and the line was still very long. We hadn't eaten lunch, and we were very hungry, but we were so excited, we almost didn't notice. While we were filming in line, some of the staff went about fifty feet behind us and cut the line off. They told the inventors beyond the cutoff to come back on Sunday to get interviewed. In the meantime, we stood in line and the crew filmed us. We had everybody's attention. The inventors waiting in line marveled at Daddy's easy mower. He was definitely the most popular inventor this day.

They finished filming us, and then we left. It was a funny sight observing an eighty-year-old man pushing a lawn mower through the lobby of the Hyatt on our way to the vehicle. We didn't go around the building and up the stairs on the sidewalk like we did early that morning because we were now celebrities; at least to us and a few of the inventors, we were celebrities. We pushed it across the carpet, past the bellhops, waving at the security guards, past the front desk on our way out to the parking deck. We thought we were something. We had a good case of the big head. Looking back, I can see how celebrities can get a false sense of their importance. We felt like we had arrived. This was our moment of stardom.

We packed the easy mower in the blazer and headed back to the Sailport Resort.

Chapter 14

Will You Buy Me a Glass of Wine?

We were about to starve. We had been feeding off emotion for hours, but now it was time to eat and celebrate. We found an expensive steak and seafood restaurant next door to our hotel room. We walked in on cloud nine.

The restaurant wasn't open yet; we were too early for that, but the bar was. We sat at the bar and waited fifteen minutes for the restaurant to open.

I tried my best to get Daddy to buy me a glass of wine in honor of our celebration. I said, "Dad, let's celebrate by you buying me a glass of wine."

He wouldn't do it.

He said, "I don't need a drunk driving because I am not going to drive."

We were only one hundred yards from our hotel room, so I didn't follow his logic. We took advantage of the time and made phone calls home instead of drinking wine.

Angela, Joan, and Mama were excited for us. They asked what seemed like twenty million questions about what went on that day and acted like we hadn't kept them abreast of the events as they occurred. Even though we called them through-out the day as events evolved, they were probably right in our lack of minute details. These three women are very adamant on details while Daddy and I are interested in the bottom line. In this case, the bottom line is we get to appear before the real judges on Monday.

We recapped the day with them once more and told them about the girl who worked for the show wanting to carry Daddy to California with her. Mama thought that wasn't funny. Mama asked, "What did she look like, Furney?" Daddy said, "She wasn't as pretty as you and nothing to worry about, sweetie." I started laughing out loud. I said, "Dad, why did you tell Mama that lie. You know that woman was smoking hot." He said, "Son, when you have been married as long as I have, you don't tell Mama everything. She is on a need-to-know basis. In this case, your Mama didn't need to know that young girl was smoking hot. Rule number one, son, for a successful marriage, if Mama ain't happy, ain't nobody happy. Rule number two, if you forget, refer back to rule number one." We finally got off the phone with the women sometime after five. Finally it was time to eat.

We sat at a table by the glass wall where we had a view of Tampa Bay. The beautiful smooth teal water was breathtaking.

I knew that Daddy's wallet was going to be lighter when we left this place because we had a waiter and a waitress serving us, both with towels laid neatly over their arms. It didn't matter about his wallet to me because I was hungry. We hadn't eaten all day, and the good news was I wasn't paying for this meal. Things were falling in place for us to eat high on the hog as my dad likes to say. We ate eighty dollars' worth of food. To some of you, that might not be an expensive meal, but for ole country folks like Dad and myself, that was expensive eating. I made sure Daddy left our servers a nice tip. We talked and ate for about an hour. We finished and made our short drive to our room at the Sailport Resort. We went up to our room and relaxed for a few minutes before our excitement overtook us. We went to the front desk and talked to Charles and others who were working, telling them we had been to the *American Inventor* auditions over at the Hyatt. Charles and one of the staff members walked with us to the Blazer where we took the easy mower out of the back and gave them a quick demonstration. They liked it.

They commented on the amount of grass there is in Florida and you cut it basically year-round. They thought the mower will be a big success.

We told them about the events of the day and that a reporter interviewed us for a story in the Sunday paper. We said that we would need at least six copies of the upcoming Sunday edition of the *Tampa Tribune*. Charles said it wouldn't be a problem getting us some extra papers.

We went back to the room and relaxed and watched TV for a little while. It was around 7:30 p.m., and Daddy began to make preparations to go to bed.

He called Mama, and I called and talked to Angela and Joan for a few minutes. I told Angela and Joan that "tightwad Daddy wouldn't even buy me a glass of wine because he didn't want a drunk driving him to the hotel." They thought that was funny. I said, "That's okay, I got him back because we ordered eighty dollars' worth of food, and plus I made him leave a twenty-dollar tip."

Daddy took his usual birdbath before he settled down for the night. I guess he was regressing back to the old days before he had a bathtub and shower in our home. He said he didn't stink. Since he wore the same outfit for three days in a row, I guess his clothes didn't smell either. In his defense, the producers told us to wear the same clothes on Monday that we wore on Saturday at the audition. They never said we had to wear the same outfit on our way home and on into the rest of the week! He also wore his contestant wristband all day Saturday, Sunday, and Monday. I finally made him take it off as we were leaving Florida Monday afternoon.

That night, Daddy went on to sleep even though it was still early. I went to the front desk and bought a Snickers bar. We had some sodas in our refrigerator from our Friday shopping spree at Walgreens, so I munched on snacks and watched TV while lying on the hide-a-bed sofa in the living room. I dozed off around 11:00 p.m.

Chapter 15

He Was Out of His Comfort Zone

I slept late on Sunday morning, but Daddy got me up at 6:40 a.m. I took a shower. Daddy and I got dressed. We drove about three miles to a diner named Nikki's. They billed it as an omelet place, but it was more like a greasy spoon; though the food was quite good. I had ham, egg, and cheese omelet and my usual coffee. Daddy had bacon, eggs, and grits. We talked about the events of the previous day. I said, "Dad, are you still excited about what happened yesterday?" He said, "Son, I feel great about our chances of winning."

I had picked up our six copies of the *Tampa Tribune* at the front desk and flipped through a copy until I found our picture and article in the paper. I read the article twice. "Dad, can you believe, they put our picture in the *Tampa Tribune*? This is a great sign. We will get a lot of exposure from this article." Dad smiled. "Wipe the grits off your chin," I said. We chuckled and sipped our coffee.

After breakfast we drove to the A La Carte Event Pavilion to get a feel for where we were going for the judging round. Chris gave us good directions, and we found the place with no problem. It was beautiful. The pavilion had a canal flowing behind the buildings, and on the other side of the canal were attractive homes. We hung out a few minutes and then drove back to the hotel.

Back in the hotel room, we chilled out and looked over the 119-question questionnaire we had to turn in on Monday prior to appearing before the judges. One of the items that had to be filled out on the application was listing six references along with their addresses and phone numbers. I called Joan and put her to work on this. She said that she would handle it.

Daddy and I continued filling out the questionnaire. I said, "Dad, it's taking a long time to fill out this questionnaire. I want some me time."

We took a break; I decided to go for a run, and Daddy said he was going for a walk. I went running across the street into an upscale commercial district filled with condos, commercial offices, gorgeous landscaping and water. The scenery was eye-catching this Sunday morning as I was enjoying my run. I made a point to enjoy every moment of this trip, and I had been persuading Daddy to do the same during this whole process.

As I was finishing up my run, coming up the driveway toward the hotel room, I happened to look up on the second-floor balcony and saw Daddy getting up off the floor. My heart sank to my feet. The first thought that came to mind was he was going to have to spend Monday in the hospital and miss the interview before the judges. What would I do? I gathered myself and hollered at Daddy and asked him, "Are you okay?"

He said, "I am fine."

I ran up the stairs to see for myself.

He said, "The couple of people who had stopped to help me have already left."

I wanted to get their side of the story, but they were long gone.

Dad said, "I had been sitting on the balcony floor for a few minutes before you came up. I was in the process of pulling myself up with the help of the porch rail when you were approaching the hotel."

We went inside and sat down for a few minutes. I asked him, "What happened?"

He said, "I had just finished my walk and was coming back to the room, when all of a sudden I felt light-headed and fell."

It was around noon and pretty hot outside, so I figured he must have gotten too hot walking. Daddy's daily routine is walking around 6:00 a.m. when the weather is cooler, so he was definitely out of his comfort zone. We got something to drink.

As I was sitting on the couch, Daddy stood up and walked toward the sliding glass doors. His back was to me. All of a sudden, he lost his balance and fell down.

"I just lost my footing," he said. I was concerned at this point. I told him to sit down and rest. I told him that I was going to go outside on the balcony for a few minutes. Then I called Joan. "Joan, I don't know what's going on with Daddy, I just came back from my run, and I saw daddy pulling himself up outside on the porch. He had fallen for no apparent reason. On top of that, we came inside and sat down. Then Daddy stood up, lost his balance, and fell down." Joan said, "Is he okay now?" I said, "Yes." She said, "What do you think caused him to fall?"

"I don't know, I will keep an eye on him and let you know. Do not tell Mama what happened."

She agreed not to tell Mama anything about this situation.

I kept an eye on him, and pretty soon I was comfortable knowing that he was going to be okay. I had diagnosed his condition as getting too hot. Joan agreed with my assessment. In a few minutes, I went swimming; Daddy stayed in the room and rested.

I messed around in the pool for around thirty minutes. I talked to some people who were vacationing. I told them I was down here with my dad to audition for the *American Inventor* show. They wished us good luck.

I got out of the pool, dried off, and went back to the room. Daddy was still resting. I took a shower and got dressed.

Joan called me about the six references that we needed to put on Daddy's application. She was running into some issues because of the way people can be peculiar and concerned about the strangest things. One of the references wanted to know what time the *American Inventor* show would call. Another reference wanted to know *American Inventor*'s phone number because they have caller ID and they don't answer calls from strange numbers. This particular reference wanted to know if *American Inventor* show had tried to call her already. Joan told them, "We haven't given them your name out yet. We are asking your permission to use your name as a reference."

Joan couldn't believe their responses. She was getting the third degree from these people.

I thought it was funny.

We left and went to the mall. Since we were getting hungry, we decided to eat Chinese food in the food court. We ate and talked for a while about the events that happened on Saturday and what we expected to happen on Monday. "Dad, I believe that we are going to woo them judges and they are going to fall in love with your easy mower." Dad said, "I believe that we will get all four judges to vote yes."

While we were eating, Joan called.

She asked, "What are you guys doing?" I told her, "We are eating Chinese and talking about the past events of the weekend." Joan said, "I got off the phone with our brother, Jacky, earlier and was telling him about the process." She told him that Daddy will be in California for six weeks. Note: my sister and I always had confidence that he was going to win in Tampa. Jacky asked her, "Do you think that Daddy was up to going to

California and staying there for six weeks?" Joan replied, "I had just talked to Randy and at that time he was swimming laps and Daddy had been on a two-mile walk. So, Jacky, what are you doing?" He said, "I am at K&W Cafeteria eating lunch." Joan said, "Oh well." My sister was implying that we were exercising and keeping ourselves in shape while my brother was stuffing his face with food. She has a way in getting the point across. I laughed at what she told Jacky. I further stated to her, "Daddy is of good shape physically, and he will be fine in California." She said, "I already knew that. That was the point I was relaying to our brother."

We hung up with Joan, finished eating, and walked through the mall to Sports Authority. We went in and bought my son, Randall, a baseball glove and basketball. We left, got into the Blazer, and drove back to the room.

Since we ate a late lunch, we didn't eat supper. We munched on some snacks later on that afternoon. Daddy called Mama before he went to bed around 8:00 p.m. I stayed up and watched TV, then called Angela and said goodnight. Before going to bed at 11:00 p.m., I made sure all the parts of the application were filled out and ready to present.

Chapter 16

Judges, Here We Come

Daddy got up around 5:00 a.m. He took his usual bird-bath and put on the same clothes he had on Saturday. The reason for doing this was they wanted to create the illusion that the sequence of events flowed together so the video would look like it happened at the same time. It made sense.

I showered, and then we took off for the A La Carte Event Pavilion. We stopped and ate breakfast at McDonald's at 6:30 a.m. We had plenty of time to kill because we were scheduled to be there at 8:00 a.m. and we were only five minutes away. As usual, Daddy was ready to leave McDonald's as soon as he finished eating. He didn't want to be late.

As we drove to the pavilion, nervous excitement overtook us. We were going to be one of the twenty-five finalists out of five hundred contestants who were going to finally get to present their invention before the panel of famous judges. It was intimidating because each one of the judges was successful in their own right.

The first judge, Peter Jones, a successful British entrepreneur, was coproducer of the *American Inventor* show along with Simon Cowell, a man known for his blunt candor as a judge for many years on *American Idol*. As a judge, Peter mimicked

Simon Cowell's demeanor. He was the skeptic who played the devil's advocate in his role as judge.

George Foreman, famous boxer and well-known inventor in his own right, was the second judge.

The third judge was Pat Croce, former owner of the Philadelphia 76ers, author, and TV sports commentator.

The final judge, Sara Blakely is known as an entrepreneur who revolutionized the panty hose industry.

We got out of our vehicle and walked to the big covered patio at the back of the building. The patio was next to a canal separating the pavilion from the gorgeous homes across the water. It was a beautiful view with lots of sunshine and excitement in the air.

We approached a table, and there were staff members who greeted us and got us registered. We had some free time since we had arrived an hour early. We got a chance to talk to some of the contestants as we were waiting to go inside of the building. At 8:00 a.m. they would start bringing the contestants inside the building to present before the judges. We were nervous and excited waiting for our turn.

We saw contestants come out of the double doors leading into the judging room. Most came out disappointed and sad because the judges had voted them down. You had to receive three yes votes in order to be considered in the final voting, which would be revealed later on in the summer on the TV show.

Finally, it was our turn.

They brought us inside into a banquet room. They interviewed and filmed us right before we were to go into the big double doors behind us. The interviewer said, "I am your coach. Here is what I want you to do. When Sara Blakely starts talking to you, make sure that you flirt with her and give her that Southern charm that you have. She will eat it up, and you will have her eating out of your hands." I thought to myself that the interviewer was joking. Looking back, Daddy must have taken that coaching advice seriously. They took the easy mower from us; it would be waiting in the dark hallway for us, which led down to the judges, and we would grab it in the hallway and make the final fifty-foot walk to the judges.

Nervous butterflies had settled in my stomach. I am not sure how Dad felt.

I looked at Daddy and said, "Let's do it."

I opened the double doors, and Dad and I made the seemly long walk down the hallway. Daddy grabbed the easy mower and pushed it toward the bright lights at the end of the hallway where the four judges were sitting, watching an eighty-year-old man pushing a lawn mower.

The bright lights and multiple cameras were focused on us. I can't imagine what they were thinking watching him push a lawn mower down the hallway. I said to myself this must be a dream. Somebody needs to pinch me and wake me up. I pulled my thoughts together and proceeded. I can't imagine what Dad was thinking.

We paused about fifteen feet in front of the table.

George Foreman spoke up and said, "Welcome, Mr. Eubanks. What do you have to show us today?" Dad said, "You can call me Furney." George said, "Okay, Furney, show us what you got." Daddy said, "My name is Furney Eubanks, and this is my son Randy. We are here today to show you our new invention which is called the easy mower. May we proceed?" All the judges nodded and George said, "Proceed."

It was kind of funny watching him pretend like he was mowing grass in the hallway. Daddy started pushing the mower back and forth in front of the table the judges were sitting at. He used the legs of the table as fake bushes around your home. He would maneuver back and forth. It was a hilarious sight watching the judges pick up their legs so Daddy wouldn't run over them. Pat Croce said, "I am glad the mower is not cranked." Everybody laughed. Daddy was focused on what he was doing. He was in his own little world. He paused pushing the mower for a minute and said, "See how easy it is to push and steer this mower. In fact, it's so easy to maneuver that even an eighty-year-old World War II veteran like myself can push it with ease." The judges looked at one another and started grinning.

Sara Blakely said, "What inspired you to invent this mower." Dad said, "I always look at how to make things and devices easier to work with. I was getting old, and I was finding it difficult to push a regular push mower. On top of that, I didn't like using a weed eater because they are hard to crank for an older man like me. I thought about it, and after three years of working in my shop, I came up with this lawn mower. It's so easy to push, and you can get close enough around buildings and bushes, you don't have to use a weed eater." Sara asked him, "What's your secret to looking so young?" I thought to myself, what does that have to do with this mower? My dad said, "I do a lot of walking and looking at pretty women like you. That's what keeps me young." I couldn't believe he said that. She grinned and said, "Furney, you are a cutie."

He went on to tell them he was a WWII vet, farmer, upholsterer, etc. He said the idea was to make grass mowing easier. The sliding deck makes it easier to get closer to buildings and shrubbery, eliminating the need for a weed eater in most cases.

"I invented it so that it would save time and energy for myself and others," he said. Dad started back with his demo. I thought to myself they probably got the idea in how it works by now.

He continued pushing and steering the mower, showing how the body of the mower would slide or glide easily around the pretend bushes in the hallway. He stated with pride and enthusiasm, "It is so easy to mow grass with this mower, that even an eighty-year-old World War II veteran can do it." I said to myself, oh my God, he is repeating himself. My dad has a habit of that.

All the judges smiled and seemed to be interested.

I remember George Foreman was extremely nice and said, "I want one of these mowers." When our short demo was finished, it was time to vote. Dad and I stood there together in front of the judges with nervous confidence.

The first judge, Pat Croce, said, "Yes."

The second judge, Peter Jones, said, "No." I thought to myself, you probably don't mow your own grass anyway.

It was George Foreman's turn, and he said, "Yes."

The drama was building. The fourth and final judge, Sara Blakely, was going to determine our fate. Her vote was going to decide whether we were going to move on to the finals and go home on cloud nine or like so many other contestants we saw returning back through the double doors with their head hanging down, revealing their look of disappointment. I whispered to Daddy, and said, "Smile at Sara like the coaches said."

The coaches had told Daddy before we entered the hallway to make sure he flirted with Sara. He didn't disappoint. My dad gave her that Southern grin.

It was her turn.

She said, "Congratulations, you are moving forward. It is a yes."

We were excited and we thanked them. It seemed like it took forever to walk the fifty feet coming in, but going out we acted like we were going to a fire sale. We were booking it. We busted through the double doors with a big grin on our faces.

Our interviewer/coach stopped us and asked, "What did the judges say?" "The judges said yes!" my dad replied. The interviewer asked Daddy, "how do you feel?" We both said,

"We feel good about our chances of winning here in Tampa and going to California." He asked what was the vote count and who put you over the top? Daddy said, "Three said yes, and one said no. Sara was the deciding vote." The coach asked, "Did you flirt with Sara?" Dad said, "I sure did, just like you told me to do." I would like to make a point here. My dad's flirting is innocent. It seems like he has been flirting a lot since he has been in Tampa. It was all in good fun. Most of it was brought on by the staff. My dad and mama have been married over sixty years, and I can assure you he has been faithful to her. She is the queen of his heart.

Other contestants congratulated us. After the interview, we went outside and were greeted by other staff members. As we were leaving the building, one lady told us, "Someone will be contacting you soon about how they would proceed from here. The next step would be the production crew coming out to your house, Mr. Eubanks, to film and interview the family and look at your other inventions and workshop." They cut his wristband off he had been wearing all weekend. I thought to myself, now maybe he would change these clothes he had been wearing all weekend, but that didn't happen.

On our way out in the parking lot, we saw our friend Bobby. Bobby had invented the commercial cake cutter. We asked him how it went before the judges. "They said no," replied Bobby. He was disappointed but happy for us. We talked for a few minutes and proceeded to our vehicle.

We loaded up the easy mower and sat in the Blazer for a few minutes contemplating what had just transpired. We were excited.

Before we took off, I called Angela. "Hello, honey, the judges said yes, we are going to be on the show, and they are coming to Trenton to interview the family and look at Daddy's inventions and workshop." She was excited for us. She said,

"The *Daily News* wants to interview your daddy." I told her, "We are still here, and I will go back in and ask if it was okay for the newspaper to interview him."

Daddy had signed a bunch of disclosure papers along with the 119-question questionnaire that we had turned in earlier, so I had my doubts about whether he could do the interview. I ran back in and asked the lady we had talked to on our way out. She said, "Absolutely not, do not talk to anyone until after the shows are aired starting in June. The final show will be in July in which they will announce the winner. Keep it a secret, the details of the interview before the judges. Don't do any newspaper interviews."

I called Angela back and told her, "We can't talk to anyone—anyone—about the show." A few minutes later, Joan called me and said, "It seems like I told three hundred people about you two going before the judges." I said, "You have to call them back and tell them not to say anything. The lady who works for the show said not to tell anyone about the judges interviewing us until after the shows are aired starting in June." I doubt if she had called three hundred people, but knowing her she had spread the word. I said, "By the way, not only were we interviewed by the judges, but we are going to be on the show. We got three yes votes and one no vote. We are going to win this thing and go to California." Joan was so excited that she couldn't contain herself. I could hear her hollering on the other end of the phone, "My daddy is going to win."

Chapter 17

Leaving with High Hopes and Optimism

We took off from Tampa heading home. We were optimistic when we started this journey five days ago, and our optimism had intensified to a new level.

But at the same time, Daddy and I had traveled down this road before, getting our hopes up in the past for other inventions he had invented. In the past, the end was always disappointment. We just knew the tool holder that Empire Brush Company had spent so much time on was going to be a big hit. Daddy and I had tested the market by making and selling them to various hardware and paint stores. But we were slapped back into reality by disappointment.

This time was going to be different; we would not be defeated by disappointment this time. No excuses, we were going to win this event in Tampa and move on to California for the grand prize. We had properly prepared for it, and we were convinced victory was a matter of time. We weren't cocky, but we were confident. Daddy and I continued our drive to our homes in eastern North Carolina.

It was getting late in the afternoon. Time passed quickly as we were talking about the events of these past few days. Daddy was planning on how to spend the money if he won.

He said, "I am going to first of all give my local church a huge contribution." Daddy continued on. "The second thing I am going to do is buy a brand-new pickup truck. It's going to be red. It will have heated leather seats and a voice speaking to me from the dashboard giving me directions. After all that is done, then I am going to put away enough money to take care of me and your mother. Lastly, I am not going to wait until I die to take care of you, Joan, and Jacky." I said, "Daddy, how much do you think it will take to care for you and Mama since you two are big spenders." He laughed and said, "You know how tight I am with my money. I figured half million dollars will take care of your mama and I the rest of our lives." Daddy loves the Lord, and he was humbled how God took care of and blessed him all these years.

It was obvious to me while talking to Daddy on this trip that he was at the age in which he was thinking about his legacy. He kept saying how he wanted to be able before he died to set his family up financially. He said, "Leaving you kids a financial inheritance is important to me."

I shared with him that what was important as far as his legacy was concerned was not money; it was his teaching and great example he had lived before his three children all these years. My dad was a pillar in the community, and he had a reputation of helping people, being friendly, and a hard worker. He never met a stranger.

He said, "Yes, I tried my best to set a good example."

But that wasn't enough; it was important to him to leave us a nest egg. One of my dad's favorite sayings is "Your actions speak so loud, I can't hear a word you are saying."

I said, "It's all good."

I believed he would get his wish, and the easy mower was going to pay off for him.

It was 4:00 p.m., and we were getting hungry because we hadn't eaten lunch. We pulled over at a Golden Corral.

Dad said, "I am feeling woozy, and I need to go to the bathroom."

He had this same problem back at the hotel room when I found him getting up off the balcony floor. I was beginning to get concerned about him.

He came out of the bathroom, and we sat down and ate.

After we ate he said, "I am feeling better."

I was not sure what was going on with him. I shrugged it off as being out of his environment and out of his routine.

I said, "Daddy, when you get back home and if these woozy spells happen again, you are going to a doctor." He said, "Okay."

The strange thing is once he got home, these woozy spells never happened again.

We got back into the Blazer and headed north. We spent the night at a Best Western in Brunswick, Georgia. The next morning, we got up, ate breakfast, and, in a few hours, pulled into Daddy's driveway. It was great to be back home.

I hung around and talked to Mama for a little while. We had to tell her all about the trip. We rehashed every detail. It was a great feeling watching with excitement as my dad told about our adventure.

As I was listening to him and absorbing the moment, I thought to myself, I accomplished my main goal of this trip: to spend six days with my dad that I will never forget. It was a success because that happened, and no matter what would transpire as far as winning the *American Inventor* contest, we wouldn't be defeated by disappointment. Disappointment can't defeat quality time spent with your dad, sharing stories, dreaming big goals together. In my opinion, that is true love.

The next few weeks were a time of anticipation and great excitement. I had multiple conversations with Angela, Joan, and my parents on what was going to happen next. None of us knew what was going to transpire. We had high hopes and dreams that we would win in Tampa and be heading to California in pursuit of the big prize. In the meantime, we had to put off newspaper interviews. The *Jones County Post*, *Daily News*, *Kinston Free Press*, *Sun Journal*, and *News & Observer*, which was two hours away in Raleigh, wanted to interview a local celebrity like my dad. We told them all they had to wait until after the last show was aired in mid-July before they could print an interview or any pictures. The newspapers understood and held off.

Chapter 18

Hollywood Comes to Dad's Workshop

That following Thursday, I got a call from Chris Licota from the *American Inventor* show in California. He said that Nick Kellis, a producer from the show, will be calling me on Friday. They will be flying out to interview and film Daddy and the family along with his other inventions at his home the following Saturday.

I called Angela, Joan, and my dad, and with every conversation, the excitement moved to a higher level. Joan was disappointed because she and Pate were going to be out of town the weekend to celebrate her birthday. My brother, Jacky, who lives in Hickory, would be unavailable to make the six-hour drive down this weekend. Angela and I would have to represent the children. Joan was concerned that I would claim that I was the only child and by my luck become a star. She was just kidding, even though she did write this in her poem later on at Daddy's celebration.

On Friday afternoon, I received a call from Nick Kellis. He and his coworker, Michael, would be flying into Raleigh in the morning. They would be driving out to see us at Daddy's house late in the afternoon and would call when he got on the road. I asked him if he wanted me to bring Angela and Randall with me for the interview. He said by all means. Randall is our youngest child and the only one living at home. Our oldest daughter, Brandy, and our middle daughter, Amanda, were grown and married. He also said to bring any other inventions that Dad had made.

The only invention that I had at my house was a plastic prototype of the tool holder that Empire Brush had hand carved years earlier by one of their engineers. The other inventions were at Daddy's workshop.

I didn't think Saturday would ever get here. Once Saturday arrived, I was eagerly waiting for Nick's call. I was just sitting around and pacing back and forth from the refrigerator to the living room. Angela told me, "Why don't you chill out. He will call you soon." It was getting past noon, and I hadn't heard anything. Joan and I talked back and forth most of the day. She kept asking, "Has Nick called you yet?" Joan, like me, has a go-getter attitude and wants things to happen now. I know we were aggravating Pate. He was looking forward to spending a romantic weekend in Beaufort, South Carolina, for Joan's birthday. Thanks to me, Angela, Jacky, Pat, and Pate's sister, Mel, Joan was on the phone most of the weekend. I thought that was funny, but I could feel his pain.

Finally, about 2:00 p.m., I got a call from Nick, and he said he was on his way and would be at Dad's house around 5:00 p.m. Angela, Randall, and I took off toward Trenton in much anticipated excitement.

We arrived at Dad's house a few minutes ahead of Nick and Michael. We were sitting in the living room waiting on them to arrive, and we were all nervous. Finally, we saw a white van pull up in the driveway. Two men got out with a camera and some other equipment. They were here!

We didn't wait for them to ring the doorbell; instead, we all rushed out, introduced ourselves, and let the fun begin.

Michael ran the camera while Nick held the microphone and asked questions. We started filming out in Daddy's workshop.

Nick asked him detailed questions about the setup and the organization of the workshop.

Dad had made homemade molds and other braces in order to bend the metal which was used on his numerous inventions. Daddy described in detail the tool holder he invented. He told Nick how we had sold more than 115 of them to various hardware and paint stores.

Dad showed him the ingenious claw hammer with the extra claw. The way he designed it you had extra leverage to pull a nail out of wood, making it easier and more efficient than a regular claw hammer.

Daddy showed Nick and Michael the plow he designed to pull behind a riding lawn mower. He didn't design the first plow to hook up behind a mower, but he improved an existing design to make it stay in the dirt without constantly popping up.

The plow reminded me of his first invention, the tobacco harvester clip. He didn't design the first clip; he just redesigned a more efficient version.

Nick was especially intrigued at the wheelchair-looking apparatus which Daddy called the elevatable workstation.

Last but not least, he asked about the easy mower. Daddy described in detail how he wanted to design a push lawn mower where you could maneuver the mowing deck close around bushes and buildings in order to eliminate using a weed eater. It was amazing watching him steer the push mower and how he could slide the mower deck close to the bushes just by twisting the handle. With a simple twist, the deck glided back and forth on small swivels, thanks to a clever attachment tied in to the steering rack.

He said, "Myself and millions of senior citizens were getting at the age in which we don't want to be aggravated in operating a weed eater that at times was difficult to crank."

They finished up filming and interviewing outside. We all went inside, and they had the family sit around the kitchen table. Nick asked all of us questions starting with Mama.

He asked her what she thought about all the countless hours he spent at night working on his inventions over the years. Mama said, "I don't understand his passion for inventing stuff, but I supported him and his inventions. I didn't interfere with his pursuits."

The questions were mainly focused on our support for Daddy and what it would mean to us if Daddy won the one-million-dollar grand prize. They filmed us as we were sitting around the table talking and answering Nick's questions. We all enjoyed the interview.

In that moment, I felt like that I needed to pinch myself to make sure this was really happening. It seemed like time was standing still. I didn't want this to end. I wanted to savor what was going on at that present time forever. What a great moment for our family.

They wrapped up the interview around 10:00 p.m. Nick and Michael were staying in Jacksonville for the night. He had no clue how to get there. I told him he could follow us and I would lead him to his hotel. We all said our goodbyes, and Nick told Daddy they would be in touch with him soon. They followed us to Jacksonville, and we found their hotel. He thanked me and promised to call me soon.

On our way to Jacksonville from Dad's, I called Joan and filled her in on all that transpired in the interview. We talked for what seemed like thirty minutes. She was so excited and asked me what I thought.

"It's going to be good," I said. "The interview went great. Nick started out filming in his workshop. We then came inside and sit around the table while Nick asked each one of us questions about Daddy and his inventions."

We kept reassuring ourselves that he was going to win the Tampa regionals and would soon be going to California. I was wound up that night and found it difficult to go to sleep. I kept rehearsing and thinking about the events of the last few hours. I was full of hope for my daddy. Needless to say, the whole family was pumped up after the production crew had flown all the way from California to film and interview Dad and the family. I can honestly say we all felt with 100 percent certainty that Daddy was at least going to win the Tampa Bay contest. This meant that he would receive fifty thousand dollars to further develop his product. I was looking forward to accompanying him to California. The only thing that was standing in our way was a confirmation from Nick.

Chapter 19

The Waiting Game

It had been almost two weeks since the interview with Nick and Michael. Daddy, along with other family members, kept asking me why we haven't heard from him yet. Finally, on Friday, May 11, I gave Nick a call.

When I got Nick on the phone, the first thing he did was thank me again for guiding him to his hotel room. He also commented on how much he enjoyed flying out and meeting the family and doing the interview. He spoke highly of Dad and wished him good luck in how this might turn out for him. He said the decision makers had to do some last-minute rearranging on their schedule. I am not sure what that meant. He further stated that it was taking a little longer than they thought to make a decision on the regional winner in Tampa. He assured me that Daddy was definitely in the running for consideration to be chosen. He said they should know something by next Tuesday.

I filled everyone in on what Nick had said. The excitement continued to build. We couldn't wait for next Tuesday to arrive.

One thing to note here, I am like my daddy in a number of ways. For example, when someone tells Daddy they are going to do something on a certain day and a certain time, he expects them to do what they say. He has always lived his life this way. I also feel the same way.

Sure enough, next Tuesday came and went without a word from Nick. Daddy called me that late afternoon and wondered what was going on. I played it off and said Nick was probably busy or they haven't made a decision yet. I told him to be patient and we would hear something soon. Not to worry, it would be good news.

Another week passed and still no word from Nick. It was now May 22, and time was running short. They had to announce the winners of the respective regionals before the first show aired on Wednesday, June 6. By now, Nick was a week late in calling us. My patience had run out, and I had enough of the suspense, so I called Nick.

Chris Licato answered the phone. I told him who I was and I was calling Nick. Chris remembered me and Dad. He said Nick was in another department. I told Chris that Daddy was getting anxious considering Nick was supposed to call him back a week ago and let him know about the final decision. Chris reassured me that the winner had not been called yet. He said that Nick would call us in a week or so and let us know one way or another. I didn't know what to think about that answer.

On the one hand, I was confident that a decision hadn't been made, and on the other hand, I felt like they weren't organized or didn't keep their word.

I immediately called Dad and reassured him that they hadn't made a decision and he would know soon. I said, "It's all good. Things will work out."

Joan, Angela, Daddy, and I were still optimistic. Mama was skeptical, and I wasn't sure how Jacky felt.

I got some good news that same Tuesday evening. Michael, who came with Nick to see Daddy three weeks ago, called me and asked me to sign a release form he was going to fax me. He forgot about it when he and Nick were at Dad's house interviewing us. To me, that was good news. I thanked him and told him as soon as I got it, I would read over it, sign, and return.

I called Daddy and said, "Guess what? Do you remember the cameraman Michael? He called me and said he was going to fax me a release form that he forgot to get us to sign when him and Nick came down." Dad said, "This is a good sign. They still must be interested in us."

The next morning, I read over the release form, signed, and faxed to Michael. That evening, Angela and I were sitting in our living room. It was around 9:30 p.m. and Mama called.

As I watched her number show up on caller ID, I told Angela, "That was late for her to be calling. They are usually in bed before now. Well, maybe not Mama, but Daddy goes to bed early."

I answered the phone and Mama said, "Daddy had just got a call from Kerry. Kerry said she was with *American Inventor*. Do you know who she is?" Before I could answer, Mama asked me, "Do you think she was legitimate?"

I told her, "That was a stupid question. Why would someone call up Daddy pretending to be with *American Inventor*? Let me speak to Daddy."

He got on the phone, and he was excited. "Kerry wanted to know my schedule for the next few days." He told her, "Mae and I are going to the eye doctor on Thursday. We will be home Friday and first of next week." He asked Kerry, "Are you bringing me good news?"

She laughed and said, "You are a mess."

Daddy was so excited that he said, "You and Mama need to get off of the phone with me so I can call Joan."

I told Mama before she got off the phone that "you needed to read the Bible. Pay attention to Hebrews 11:1 (NKJV), 'Faith is the substance of things hoped for, the evidence of things not seen.'"

I was referring to her negative comment if Kerry was legitimate and her seemingly lack of faith.

Daddy asked me, "Do you remember Kerry?"

I didn't remember any of the ladies we had met in Tampa except Lacy. After I hung up the house phone, I turned on my cell phone and brought it upstairs with me to the bedroom. I knew Joan would be calling me after Daddy finished talking to her.

Angela and I were in bed watching the *Ellen Show*, which we had taped. In a few minutes, Joan called. She was excited.

She asked me, "What do you think?"

I picked on her and told her, "Kerry was fake," as a reference to Mama's comment.

In just a moment, Jacky called her. Joan said, "Hang on, Randy, Jacky is on the other line."

She was talking to him on the landline and me on the cell phone. Joan talked a few minutes and said, "I have got to get off and watch the end of *American Idol*."

After that, Jacky called me and asked, "Do you think that Daddy is mentally up to traveling to California and going through this process?"

I told him, "Jacky, you are sounding like Mama. Daddy will be fine."

The next morning at 8:30 a.m., I got a call from Joan. She said, "I had to take Nyquil to go to sleep last night because I was too excited to sleep. I believe they might surprise Daddy on Friday."

The hype was building up. As per Kerry's phone call, we had declared Daddy the winner of the Tampa regionals. She had basically confirmed it by calling Daddy and wanting to know his schedule for the next few days. That statement from her confirmed to us that they will be flying out and telling Daddy that he had won and presenting him with a fifty-thousand-dollar check. I was already starting to plan on the trip with Daddy to California.

All day Thursday, this was the only thing I could think about.

Friday finally arrived, and I was waiting for Daddy to call me and say that the *American Inventor* had called to say they were going to fly out and see him. That's how they announced the winners of each region. They would fly out to the respected winner's house and knock on their door and present them with a check.

That moment didn't happen on Friday. Or Saturday. Or Sunday or Monday or any other day the rest of that week.

We didn't know what to think. Maybe they were making the final arrangements and it was taking time to get this done?

The family didn't know what to think, and Mama was especially skeptical. We kept positive and said no news is good news, but we also knew that time was running out. They had to inform the winners before the first show would air next Wednesday. Daddy asked me if I thought that he should call them up. I said no. They will be in touch.

Chapter 20

The Decision Is Made

Sure enough, the following Tuesday, June 5, I got a call from an out-of-state number early in the afternoon. I recognized it as a California area code and was excited to answer the call. My hope was at an all-time high.

I said, "Hello," and on the other end of the call was our buddy Nick Kellis.

We talked a few minutes, and he said, "They made a decision late last night. Our decision was to go in a different direction."

I was speechless. I said, "Do what?"

I couldn't believe what he was saying.

Nick said, "It was a hard decision and your Daddy was in the running until the very end."

Disappointment had reared its ugly head again.

I told Nick, "It doesn't seem like Daddy can catch a break. He has worked so hard and put so much time in this project. Nick, Kerry called Daddy back on May 24 and told him that they would be out to see him in a few days. She wanted to know his schedule. That insinuated to us that Daddy had won."

I thought to myself that this is unprofessional and misleading.

He apologized and asked, "Did she call him back?"

I said, "No."

He said, "The Tampa show will air sometime in mid-July."

He further stated, "We have the right to manufacture the product up to three months after the show is broadcast, if a manufacturer sees it on TV and is interested in building it."

He also said, "It will be a long shot for the show to produce it, but anything is possible."

At that point I wasn't getting my hopes up.

Considering Nick said that they made their final decision last night, I believe that they had initially decided on Daddy as the winner, hence the telephone call from Kerry. I also believe they changed their mind last night as per Nick's comment. Who knew for sure?

I did know this: Daddy was going to be disappointed.

In fact, the whole family was going to be disappointed.

Nick said, "I sure was dreading making this phone call to you." He thanked me for our hospitalility.

We hung up.

I started thinking about this situation, and in a few minutes, I called Nick back. I asked him, "Would you call Daddy and tell him the news? I think it would be best if you told Daddy. I don't have the heart to do it." Besides that, Nick owed Daddy the phone call since, in my opinion, my daddy was misled.

I am not one for whining, but, wow, this was heartbreaking.

I told Angela, "Nick told me they decided to go in a different direction." She encouraged and reminded me, "There are other avenues available to move this product." She suggested, "We all need to continue helping him try to sell it."

I agreed.

It will be a while before we can help him considering they have three months of rights to it after the last show is aired.

I thought to myself, I hope and pray that my dad doesn't get discouraged. I know he will be disappointed.

I sure dreaded calling Joan and telling her. She will be disappointed also. We had all put so much work in this project with our dad. All the preparation in filling out paperwork, researching patents, getting videos made, and all the other work. It now seemed like a waste of time.

I got myself together and started thinking. This bad news does not take away from the time my dad and I spent together on our trip to Florida. We will get over this and regroup. That mower will be manufactured. We will not be discouraged.

I was still at the office when Mama called me around 6:00 p.m.

She said, "We had been away from home and just got back. Nick has left your daddy a message, and Furney had just returned the call. Nick told your daddy that he was in there to the very end, but they decided to go with someone else."

I asked to speak with Daddy. "Dad, how are you feeling?"

He said, "I am disappointed but not discouraged."

I told him, "You will get great exposure from the show and someone will manufacture it."

After I hung up with Dad, I locked up the office and went home. I figured Joan would call me, but I needed to clear my head, so I told Angela, "I am going jogging."

When I got back, Angela told me, "Joan has called you twice." Joan had told Angela, "I feel like I am at a funeral."

I didn't call her back that night. I wasn't in the mood to talk about it.

The next morning Joan called me as I was taking Randall to school and I said, "I will call you back when I drop Randall off."

I called her back, and we talked for a long time. I said, "I wonder what went wrong? Maybe they thought Daddy was too old and didn't fit the mold for who they wanted to showcase in California? Who knows, but I think he was misled by the show." Joan said, "I believe they misled him also, but things always work out for the best. Something better will come out of this for Daddy." We both agreed that when it was all said and done that Daddy was going to get great exposure out of the show and his mower would be manufactured.

She was going to call Mama, Daddy, and Jacky to get them to agree along with us that something good was coming out of this. Daddy's mower will be sold, and he won't even have to go to California.

Before I got off the phone with Joan, we prayed and spoke blessings to God for Nick and the rest of the staff at the *American Inventor* show. All will turn out well.

We decided we would have a party at Joan's house on Sunday to celebrate all that Daddy and I accomplished while in Florida. Joan and I agreed that we will do everything we can to help Daddy get his mower sold.

Chapter 21

Daddy's Celebration Party

Sunday arrived, and we all gathered at Joan's house for Daddy's celebration. Dad was dressed sharp in a shirt and tie; the rest of us dressed casual.

Besides my wife, Joan is the best hostess that I know. She went all out for Dad. She had balloons and fancy tablecloths. There was food and dessert. She made a sign that read "Daddy Is The Real American Inventor."

Mama, Joan, Pate, Jacky, Pat, Angela, Amanda, Randall, and I gathered to honor Daddy, and honor him we did. Jacky spoke about Dad's legacy and example that he set for us by his perseverance and work ethic over the years.

I read a few pages of notes that I had taken while on our trip to Florida. You are reading these notes in this book now.

Joan wrote a poem that says it all. Her poem was inspired by my son, Randall Eubanks.

It was an emotional time. We shed tears, and you would think that Daddy had won the Nobel Peace Prize or an Academy Award for best inventor. I can honestly say this was probably one of those moments that we felt a strong family bond. We were very proud of our dad.

My Grandfather Is The American
Inventor
By
Joan Phillips
Inspired By Randall Eubanks

The Golden Corral was a place we had not dined in a while.
But an early March Saturday morning "The Phillips" & "Eubanks" showed
Up In style; Our mission was on each & everyones' mind,
The best way to make Furney & his "Easy Mower" shine.

So Furney and his lovely Mae began to chat, and all
were attentive & present and from Hickory came Jacky & Pat.

It was decided that Angela & Kids would sacrifice my
younger brother, to accompany & coach our Dad & his "Easy Mower."
So after Joan made sure the applications to enter were complete,
Randy & Furney left for Tampa in Randys' Blazer that Daddy said had
Comfortable seats.

Now Matt (the attorney-to-be) grandson wondered why Tampa Bay?
Knowing that strip clubs & food was the only thing there, "Grandma";
So they say ? ? ? ? ? ? ? ?

With cell phones buzzing back and forth that soon
became a "Eubanks" tradition, Randy & Furney had great News
from Tampa making thru the 1st & 2nd Auditions.
Joan & Angela shared with a few hundred people
they knew, and Jacky, of course, between meetings & not knowing
how to use his voicemail shared with about two. A
call came from Randy to stop spreading the word. Angela
called Joan and Joan called her Mom, Pat and Mel
and they all thought "this is absurd".

- 2 -

But Monday came of that Audition weekend & oh what a thrill
Furney was a TAMPA BAY Finalist & got a yes from George
Foreman (who invented a grill).

Now on with the quest & Joan & Pate soon departed,
to Beaufort, South Carolina to have a birthday/ romantic
weekend and again it started. Cell phones were
buzzing between Randy, Angela, Jacky, Pat, Mel & Joan; &
Pate (my darling) bless his heart, set there & began to moan.

The California team with camera & crew came to Furney's
house on a mission; So Randy, Angela & Randall (the
youngest grandson) joined Furney & Mae in fashion tradition.
Jacky & Joan looked & gazed from afar,
Hoping that Randy would not claim as being the only child
and by just his luck become a star.

After five hours or so the crew pulled away; In confidence
they told Furney we will come another day. But not too
soon before Randall had a chance on film to say;
"My GRANDFATHER Is The American Inventor"

AND THAT ENDED A WONDERFUL DAY . . .

Now a lot of time has passed & Furney was told,
California "we assumed" was where he was going to get the "GOLD"
But today we celebrate & are confident that
"God" has a better way,

And that, of course, is the publicity that will be confirmed in
TAMPA BAY . . -

· 3 ·

So here's to you Furney Eubanks, "Inventor of "The Easy Mower" and Mae. Isn't it great that California did not steal you away.

American Inventor in Tampa Bay will be used to nationally get the word out . . . .

And end result "Easy Mower" will be manufactured. With that your wife, children, grandchildren (soon to be great grandchild), great grandchildren & friends . . . . . .

Have No Doubt . . .

Congratulations !! Congratulations !!

Congratulations

Congratulations !!

We love you & are so very proud of you .

June 10, 2007

My Grandfather is The "American Inventor"
Written by Joan Phillips
Inspired by Randall Eubanks

The Golden Corral was a place we had not dined in a while.
But an early March Saturday morning "The Phillips" & "Eubanks" showed
Up in style; Our mission was on each & everyones' mind,
The best way to make Furney & his "Easy Mower" shine.

So Furney and his lovely Mae began to chat, and all
Were attentive & present and from Hickory came Jacky & Pat.
It was decided that Angela & kids would sacrifice my
Younger brother; to accompany & coach our DAD & his "Easy Mower."
So after Joan made sure the applications to enter were complete,
Randy & Furney left for Tampa in Randy's Blazer that DADDY said had comfortable seats.

Now Matt (the attorney-to-be) grandson wondered why Tampa Bay?
Knowing that strip clubs & food was the only thing there, "Grandma";
So they say???????

With cell phones buzzing back and forth that soon
Became a "Eubanks" tradition, Randy & Furney had great news
From Tampa making thru the 1st & 2nd auditions.
Joan & Angela shared with a few hundred people
They knew; and Jacky, of course, between meetings & not knowing
How to use his voicemail shared with about two. A
Call came from Randy to stop spreading the word. Angela

Called Joan and Joan called her Mom, Pat and Mel
And they all thought "this is absurd".

But Monday came of that Audition weekend & oh what a thrill
Furney was a <u>Tampa Bay Finalist</u> & got a yes from George
Foreman (who invented a grill).

Now on with the quest & Joan & Pate soon departed,
to Beaufort, South Carolina to have a birthday/romantic
weekend and again it started. Cell phones were
buzzing between Randy, Angela, Jacky, Pat, Mel & Joan; &
Pate (my darling) bless his heart, sat there & began to moan.

The California team with camera & crew came to Furney's
House on a mission; so Randy, Angela & Randall (the
Youngest grandson) joined Furney & Mae in fashion tradition.
Jacky & Joan looked & gazed from afar,
Hoping that Randy would not claim as being the only child
And by just his luck become a star.
After five hours or so the crew pulled away; In confidence
They told Furney we will come another day. "But not too
Soon before Randall had a chance on film to say;
<u>"My Grandfather Is The American Inventor"</u>

And that ended a wonderful day...

Now a lot of time has passed & Furney was told,
California "we assumed" was where he was going to get the
<u>"Gold"</u>
But today we celebrate & are confident that
<u>"God"</u> has a better way,
And that, of course, is the publicity that will be confirmed in Tampa
Bay...

So, here's to you Furney Eubanks, "Inventor
of "The Easy Mower" and Mae. Isn't it
great that California did not steal you away.

American Inventor in Tampa Bay will be used
To nationally get the word out....

And end result "Easy Mower" will be manufactured.
With that your wife, children, grandchildren
(soon to be great grandchild), great grandchildren &
friends ...

Have No Doubt...
Congratulations!! Congratulations!! Congratulations!!
We love you
&
are so very proud
of you.

June 10, 2007

I believe we made him feel good. This was a proud moment in his life. I know it was the proudest moment in my life. In fact, I can speak for the whole family and say we were all proud of him. For the next seven weeks, we watched the *American Inventor* every Wednesday night. Our favorite episode was of course on July 11. That was the night that the whole nation got to see Daddy and me on TV.

As Angela and I were watching the show, it was hard to believe that there we were demonstrating a lawn mower for the whole nation to see. That was exciting. It's amazing even ten years later, I still run into someone occasionally who mentions to me that they saw Dad and me on TV.

After this show was aired, all the local newspapers featured articles and pictures of Dad. On many of them, he was on the front page. He was featured in the *Daily News* in Jacksonville, the *Free Press* in Kinston, the *Sun Journal* in New Bern, the *Tideland News* in Swansboro, the *Jones Post* in Trenton, the *News & Observer* in Raleigh, and *Farm Show Magazine*, whose main office is in Lakeland, Minnesota. *Farm Show Magazine* is distributed to farmers all over the country. He was even interviewed as a featured guest on the radio program *Down East Show*.

North Carolina General Assembly
Senate

SENATOR HARRY BROWN
6TH DISTRICT

OFFICE ADDRESS: 515 LEGISLATIVE OFFICE BUILDING
300 N. SALISBURY STREET
RALEIGH, NC 27603-5925
TELEPHONE: (919) 715-3034
(919) 754-3250 FAX
EMAIL: harryb@ncleg.net
DISTRICT: 2223 N. MARINE BLVD.
JACKSONVILLE, NC 28546
TELEPHONE: (910) 347-3777
(910) 347-1080 FAX

COMMITTEES:

APPROPRIATIONS BASE BUDGET
APPROPRIATIONS SUBCOMMITTEE ON TRANSPORTATION
AGRICULTURE
JUDICIARY I
MENTAL HEALTH & YOUTH SERVICES
OPPORTUNITIES AND NEEDS FOR ECONOMIC GROWTH IN
NORTH CAROLINA, "ONE NC"
SELECT COMMITTEE ON HOMELAND SECURITY,
EMERGENCY MANAGEMENT & MILITARY AFFAIRS

July 23, 2007

Dear Furney,

I thoroughly enjoyed reading the article about your newest invention, the Easy Mower, in a recent edition of the *Jones Post*. It sounds like you spent countless hours perfecting the mower and I'm sure that you are justifiably proud of the finished product.

Congratulations on being chosen to introduce your mower on the T.V. show, "American Inventor." I wish you every success with the show and, hopefully, the production of the Easy Mower.

Sincerely,

Harry Brown

Chapter 22

Our Last Hope

Daddy and his mower got plenty of publicity. We kept hoping as time passed that someone would see his invention on TV and call him. That never happened.

We kept trying to contact different companies. We found Dad different manufacturers on the Internet. He would call them, and most of them were owned by businesses that he had contacted years prior to being on the *American Inventor* show. Finally, in August of 2010, hope sprung back up. Briggs & Stratton was willing to give us a shot.

Daddy was put in contact with David Tiedeman, head engineer for product development with Briggs & Stratton out of the Georgia office. Here we went on another road trip, which took place in August. Our destination was McDonough, Georgia, just outside of Atlanta. The goal was to take the easy mower and demonstrate it before David Tiedeman.

I arrived at Daddy's house around 8:30 a.m. in preparation for our trip.

Of course, Mama had to put her two cents in telling me how to pack the suitcases in the car. "Why don't you put the suitcases this way and you will have more room."

I laughed and said, "We will survive without your input."

She was trying to be helpful or bossy, I'm not sure which, but you will have to ask my dad about that. We didn't waste much time. Fifteen minutes after I arrived at Dad's house, we were in the car heading to Georgia.

I was looking forward to taking this trip with Dad. This trip would be much shorter than our adventure three years earlier when we went to Tampa, Florida. In fact, we were driving down today, planned to spend the night then get up early the next morning and meet with the engineer before heading home.

Oh, by the way, we packed the easy mower in the trunk of dad's vehicle, and I also brought the famous million-dollar adjustable wrench that saved our butts when the rear right side of the mower separated from the main frame while pushing it along the cobblestoned sidewalk in Tampa, Florida, when we auditioned for the *American Inventor* show.

The conversation soon began, and it was good. Just like our trip before, Dad wouldn't shut up. I had to interrupt him to get a word in edgeways. My dad was always hopeful about a company buying one of his inventions. Like he did on our trip to Florida, he said that he was going to divide up the money from the sale of the easy mower equally between the three children after he had put away enough money to take care of him and Mama.

I told him not to worry about that, just focus on taking care of him and Mama. Dad was at the stage of his life that he was thinking a lot about his legacy. He was focusing on leaving a monetary legacy to his children. There is nothing wrong with wanting to do that. All good parents should want to leave their children money. We all want the best for our kids and help them anyway we can, but I got the feeling that Dad would be disappointed if he wasn't able to leave his kids set up financially.

I told him, let's enjoy the moment and not be worrying about leaving an inheritance.

To say the least he was excited. And he should have been. Here he was, an eighty-three-year-old man still contributing to society and chasing the American Dream of making it big. Just like most of us in this country, we have the freedom to work, produce, and pursue anything we want in this life. My dad reminded me of other Americans such as Colonel Sanders, founder of Kentucky Fried Chicken, and countless others who became financially secure in their later years and made it big.

Dad kept saying, "Briggs & Stratton will build this mower."

I looked at my clock; it was 1:00 p.m. Dad and I were getting hungry. We pulled over at Quincy Steak House for lunch. Soon afterward we were back on the road.

In a few hours we arrived at our destination: McDonough, Georgia. We checked in at the Best Western and went up to our room. By now we were getting hungry again. We walked across the parking lot and ate supper at Applebee's. When we were finished eating supper, it was Daddy's bedtime. We came back to the room, and Dad shortly went to bed, anticipating our meeting the next morning with Dave Tiedeman.

I watched TV and soon went to sleep.

Dad was up at 5:30 a.m. He took his usual birdbath and put on the same clothes he had on the day before. That wasn't surprising to me. I remembered he wore the same clothes three days in a row when we went to Tampa, Florida. I showered and we packed up. We checked out of the hotel room and were on our way to eat breakfast.

The Briggs & Stratton offices opened up at 8:00 a.m., but when you go somewhere with Daddy, being late is something he doesn't tolerate, so we drove up to the office at 7:40 a.m. The office wasn't opened yet, so we went back to the car.

At 8:00 a.m. sharp, Dad said, "Let's try again."

We walked through the door and approached the reception desk. We told the young lady that we have an appointment with Dave Tiedeman. She paged him, and in a few minutes he came out to greet us.

Dave turned out to be easy to talk to, and we bonded instantly.

He said, "Let's see your mower." We went outside, and I retrieved the easy mower from the trunk of the car.

Now, Briggs & Stratton's facilities were very professional looking and their landscaping was pristine, but lucky for us, the grass needed mowing and Dave wanted to see a demonstration. Dad cranked the mower and started in on the grass.

It was quite obvious that Dave was impressed at this concept. Dave even did his own demonstration with the easy mower. Dave said, "I like this design."

When all was said and done, Dave asked, "Can you leave the mower with me?" He told us, "Briggs & Stratton not only manufactures and sells mowers in the United States, but they have offices worldwide. I believe this mower potentially could be sold here and overseas."

We talked in the parking lot close to an hour.

Dave said, "We will take this mower and make a replica of it that would be a prototype of a finished product in which we would consider manufacturing."

We agreed to leave the mower with him.

We left McDonough, Georgia, that morning full of hope and excitement. Once again, someone had given us hope that the easy mower would be built. It was a short eight-hour trip back to North Carolina.

We reminisced all the way back home about what had just occurred. Dad was excited and so was I. We talked and imagined the easy mower being sold all over the world. The possibilities were unlimited.

Of course, we called our family members on the way back home about our conversation with Dave. Angela, Joan, and Jacky were excited for us. Mama was cautiously excited.

Over the coming months, Daddy and I corresponded with Briggs & Stratton; Daddy would call Dave by phone, and I e-mailed him. They kept the mower for over two and half years. We were hopeful the whole time. We were nervously excited.

Just like Dave promised, they made a prototype of the easy mower. Dave e-mailed me pictures, and I showed Daddy. During the process, they gave us hope that they were going to build it. They took the prototype and presented it before focus groups. Various departments in the company analyzed it. The marketing department kept it for a few months. They presented it before the production department, and they analyzed the cost of making the mower. After the prototype was built, it was basically out of the hands of Dave who was in the engineering department.

It was a little difficult for Dave to keep up with the stages of the mower since he had passed it on, but we finally got the news. They decided not to build it.

Once again, disappointment had reared its ugly head. This ended a fifty-seven-year adventure of my dad inventing things.

Easy mower (left), Briggs & Stratton prototype (right)

BRIGGS&STRATTON CORPORATION

POST OFFICE BOX 702, MILWAUKEE, WI 53201-0702 USA
P 414 259 5333

April 8, 2013

Furney Eubanks
442 Plantation Road
Trenton, NC 28585

Dear Mr. Eubanks:

Thank you for your allowing us to consider your "Easy Mower" invention. The translating handle and axle is an interesting concept to improve lawn mower maneuverability.

While we had initial interest in your invention, further review and changes in our strategies with regard to the lawn mower business has brought us to the conclusion that this concept does not meet future needs for our business. Pursuant to the 2010 Submission Agreement and Mutual Confidentiality Agreement, we are ceasing our activities associated with this concept. Your provided prototype has been returned to you and the prototype developed at Briggs & Stratton has been destroyed (see enclosed photographs).

Thank you again for your idea submission.

Sincerely,

Douglas Shears
Manager, Global Technology & Innovation
Briggs & Stratton Corporation
Research & Development

enc.

Chapter 23

Dad's Legacy Will Live On

Daddy has five patents in the Washington, DC, Patent Office, and he hasn't made a dime on any of them. The only one he made money on was the five hundred dollars he received from Long Manufacturing for his tobacco harvester clip, his first invention, back in 1956.

He has invested thousands of dollars over the years in attorney and patent fees. He has invested thousands of hours in designing these products. He wasn't concerned about the money and time he invested into his inventions. My dad's main driving force in inventing different items over the years was his desire to make people's lives easier.

I think he must have had his future son in mind when he invented the tobacco harvester clip in 1956. I am wondering if he was thinking, "I might have children one day who will be walking behind a tobacco harvester picking up all those leaves that these inferior harvester clips are dropping."

Who knows what he was thinking?

I do know this. He invented the attachment to pull behind a riding mower to hook up a pushing mower in order to save time and make his life easier as far as mowing grass. I was no longer living at home, so he designed a way to speed up his time mowing grass.

How about the times he would come to my jobsites and observe my painters working? He must have been thinking, "How can I save my son time and help him increase his profits? I can help my son and his employees become more efficient." He invented for me the elevatable workstation, the multipurpose tool holder, and a button to attach to a roller pole when we broke them off.

He was thinking about other senior citizens when he invented the easy mower.

He said to himself, "I am getting old, and I don't want to bother with having to crank a weed eater. I am one of many senior citizens who still mow their grass and struggle with pushing a lawn mower and cranking a weed eater."

So, what did he do about it?

He invented a push mower that you steer like a car and can maneuver it close to bushes and other objects, in essence eliminating the need of a weed eater for close-up trimming.

Dad has always thought about the other person's needs above his own.

My question is this: has he wasted his time?

As of today, he is ninety-one years old. He was working in his shop tinkering on stuff up until the last four years. He and Mama are currently spending their golden years in an assisted living facility. The easy mower is collecting dust inside the storage building behind my house. I have the plastic prototype of the tool holder that Dad invented and that Empire Brush redesigned inside of my safe. I have Dad's original Tobacco Harvester Clip he designed back in 1956. These items are priceless to me.

Dad's workshop where he made these inventions over the years was sold along with his home in order to help pay for his expenses at the assisted living facility.

You might ask, what's the use? Was his effort wasted?

I say not.

Here's what I have learned from his example over the years: It's great to see our elderly contributing to society and still involved in the creative process. Most people that I know who are retired take it easy. They play golf, go fishing or, worse, sit around the house and watch TV all day. They get bored. They act like life is over. They have paid their dues. They over-relax. Their actions say, "I have nothing valuable to give to society. I am too old." My dad's actions give me hope as I get older that I can still contribute and make a difference in someone's life.

We all experience discouragement and disappointment in this life. That's just the way it is. At times we want to quit and give up. Someone needs to see you get up and try again. They are depending on you to set an example of hope for them.

My dad has had his share of disappointments.

In 1956, my dad invented a harvester clip which he was told he was two years too late on this invention.

In 1989, Empire Brush Company was one of the biggest manufacturers in the country for brooms, mops, and handheld industrial tools. They spent over ten thousand dollars in turning Daddy's tool holder into a plastic prototype. They told him that they wanted to build it and pay him royalties. He knew he had hit the jackpot. At the last minute, the man in charge of research and development got promoted and the new guy who came in dropped the project altogether.

Dad was disappointed and discouraged, but what did he do? He went back to work and invented a plow to pull behind a lawn mower. Companies like Sears, Murray, Lowes, Home Depot, and Husqvarna showed interest but never came through. Dad was disappointed and discouraged.

What did he do? He modified a claw hammer, invented a button on a painter's roller pole. No company showed interest.

What did he do? He went back to work and invented the easy mower. Dad and I auditioned and appeared on the

American Inventor show. After the audition in Tampa, they came to his house in North Carolina and filmed his numerous inventions and interviewed and filmed the family. One of the producers implied that he would be a finalist and win the fifty-thousand-dollar prize for the region and be going to California to compete for the prize of one million in hopes that his mower would be mass-produced across the country. At the last minute another producer called him and said it was a hard decision, but he would not be going to California. Dad was disappointed and discouraged.

What did he do? He went back to work and submitted his mower to several other companies. In 2010, Dad and I drove to Georgia to show his mower to the chief engineer for Briggs & Stratton. They were interested in building it and kept his mower for two and one half years. They spent lots of money building a factory prototype and testing it. What happened? They decided not to build it.

What did he do? He kept plugging away throughout the years until his health told him it was time to stop.

He didn't give up when discouragement and disappointment tried to set in as a result of companies not wanting to build his inventions such as the tool holder, garden plow, elevation station for painters, paint can holder, unique-designed claw hammer, the easy mower, and others he designed.

My dad didn't give up even when his own father discouraged him from venturing out on his own. My granddaddy was a major reason my father didn't take the job offer from Mr. Long back in 1956. Even though my dad was the youngest child, he was the motivator who got things done, and my granddaddy knew it. He told Daddy if he quit farming, he would sell the farm. He put pressure on my daddy to stick around and run things. My dad's entrepreneur spirit eventually prevailed, and in the late 1960s he made the move to get out of farming and pursue a career in the upholstery business.

He told Granddaddy that the farm wasn't big enough to support his family along with his two brothers and their families.

Dad became very successful in the upholstery business despite the lack of my grandfather's blessing. He built a loyal customer following by providing excellent craftsmanship with impeccable customer service. His upholstery shop provided him the income to finance and patent his many inventions.

My granddaddy lived across the street from us. When Dad decided to quit farming, it was months before Granddaddy would speak to him and visit Daddy in his upholstery shop. My granddaddy even got mad at my father when he built a house across the street and put in an indoor bathroom.

My granddaddy, whom I loved dearly, was in some cases a very selfish man. Thank God, my dad didn't adopt the philosophy of his father concerning how he encouraged us. Dad always supported his children to venture out and pursue our dreams. Dad taught us how to overcome disappointment and to strive to be the best we can be in the face of opposition and obstacles.

My dad taught me these things by his actions. The only person you have control over is yourself. You can control your next thought, move, and plan of action.

My dad's favorite saying is "Your actions speak so loud, I can't hear a word you are saying." My dad is always thinking about others. He told me the story about when he was drafted into the Army during World War II. He said, "Son, back then when you were signing up for the draft, there was an exception if you were the youngest male child in a family that owned a farm because farmers were important in the war effort. Since my older brothers were currently serving in the Army, I could have been exempt from serving if I had chosen. Your granddaddy asked me if I wanted to opt out of being drafted." My dad said, "Who am I to be exempt? If they don't choose me, they will go down the road and pick my neighbor to go. It is my duty to serve." That's my dad, a true American hero.

Many people had no positive role model at home to set the proper example. That's no excuse for not trying again. Don't blame anyone else and give them power. Take personal responsibility and change what you can, which is you. Feel free to borrow my dad as an example to you.

Being average has never caught anyone's attention. The average person gives up. My dad is not average. He's lived a life of significance even though his inventions never paid off financially. His example of pursuing your dreams, not giving up, and holding on to hope is his legacy to his children and people who know him. You can start today by plugging away to create the same legacy my dad did.

I will leave you with this final thought. Dad wouldn't want anyone to be downhearted because he is spending his golden years at the assisted living facility. Don't think for one minute just because his workshop is sold and his tools are gone that he has quit thinking of how to make things better for people. He still has a sharp brain. Rumor has it that recently he was on one of his morning walks down the long hallway at the facility when he approached a lady in her wheelchair stroking the wheels with both of her hands in a frantic pace. Dad stopped her and said in his sweet Southern charm, "Ma'am, if you would allow me, I want to borrow that wheelchair for a few days and take it down to the maintenance shop here at the facility. When I bring it back, you will be surprised."

Daddy said, "Let me work on it. I will make your life easier." Sound familiar?

"When I get through modifying this wheelchair, it will be so easy to use that even a ninety-one-year-old man like myself might want one."

I proudly proclaim, "My dad is the smartest seventh grader on earth."

About the Author

Randy J. Eubanks was born and raised in eastern North Carolina on a small farm near Trenton. He was raised to work hard starting at the age of six years old, picking up leaves behind a tobacco harvester. He started his first business when he was twenty-one years old. Since then he has owned and operated multiple businesses. He is currently pursuing his lifelong passion of inspiring and motivating people by teaching them how to empower themselves to take personal responsibility for the outcomes of their lives. He also works as a commercial insurance sales agent.

Randy is a motivational speaker and former member of Toastmasters International where he won various speaking contests. He enjoys speaking and sharing lessons learned over the years from owning various businesses, in building relationships and personal experiences in applying various philosophies of wisdom. He graduated from Coastal Carolina Community College with an associate of arts degree in accounting and business. He earned a business of science degree in business administration from the University of North Carolina at Wilmington.

Randy has been married to his high school sweetheart, Angela, for forty years. They have two daughters and a son. They have two adorable grandchildren. His other passions include spending time with his family, especially his grandchildren. He enjoys exercising regularly by running and lifting weights. Randy and his wife reside in Jacksonville, North Carolina. He can be contacted at randyeubanks@ec.rr.com

CPSIA information can be obtained
at www.ICGtesting.com
Printed in the USA
FFHW022034181118
49396187-53801FF

9 781642 148794